Advanced Supply Chain Management

Other Books by Charles C. Poirier

Supply Chain Optimization

Business Partnering for Continuous Improvement

Avoiding the Pitfalls of Total Quality Management

Advanced Supply Chain Management

How to Build a Sustained Competitive Advantage

CHARLES C. POIRIER

Berrett-Koehler Publishers, Inc.
San Francisco

Berrett-Koehler Publishers, Inc.
450 Sansome Street, Suite 1200
San Francisco, CA 94111-3320
Tel: (415) 288-0260   Fax: (415) 362-2512
www.bkpub.com

ORDERING INFORMATION

Individual sales. Berrett-Koehler publications are available through most bookstores. They can also be ordered direct from Berrett-Koehler at the address above.

Quantity sales. Special discounts are available on quantity purchases by corporations, associations, and others. For details, contact the "Special Sales Department" at the Berrett-Koehler address above.

Orders for college textbook/course adoption use. Please contact Berrett-Koehler Publishers at the address above.

Orders by U.S. trade bookstores and wholesalers. Please contact Publishers Group West, 1700 Fourth Street, Berkeley, CA 94710. Tel: 510-528-1444; Fax: 510-528-3444.

Printed in the United States of America
Printed on acid-free and recycled paper that is composed of 50% recycled fiber, including 10% postconsumer waste.

Library of Congress Cataloging-in-Publication Data

Poirier, Charles C., 1936–
    Advanced supply chain management : how to build a sustained competitive advantage / Charles C. Poirier.
        p.   cm.
    Includes index.
    ISBN 1-57675-052-3 (alk. paper)
    1. Business logistics.   2. Production management.   3. Industrial procurement.   4. Materials management.   5. Inventory control.
    6. Physical distribution of goods.   7. Marketing channels.
    I. Title.
    HD38.5.P637   1999
    658.7'2—dc21   98-48344
                                                              CIP

First Edition

03 02 01 00   10 9 8 7 6 5 4

Book Production: Pleasant Run Publishing Services
Composition: Classic Typography

Contents

Preface

For ten years, my associates and I have studied more than two hundred global businesses in an effort to understand optimal supply chain integration. The studies were conducted with medium to large corporations seeking to gain an advantage in their markets. We also conducted research into how companies build optimized supply networks. Such organizations included raw material suppliers ConAgra, Georgia-Pacific, Tate & Lyle, Archer Daniels Midland, Du Pont, Monsanto, Occidental Chemical, Champion Paper, and Dow. Manufacturing organizations were represented by Rubbermaid, Allied-Signal, Navistar, Sun Microsystems, Corning, General Motors, Whirlpool, Sara Lee, Revlon, Nestlé, Campbell's Soup, Kimberly-Clark, Tenneco, Black & Decker, and Procter & Gamble. Distribution organizations included Alliant Food Service, Cott International, Becton-Dickinson, Lanier International, Chiquita Banana, Unisource, Spartan Stores, Baxter Healthcare, Zellerbach, Bunzl, Fleming, and SuperValu. Retailers included Sears, Pep Boys, Safeway, Kroger, Pier 1, HEB Foods, Home Depot, Auto Zone, Office Max, Wal-Mart, and Kmart. Transportation firms assisting the flow of deliveries for many of these organizations included Federal Express,

Burlington Northern, Union Pacific, Roadway Logistics, and Schneider Logistics.

These firms represent a cross-section of supply chains, initially concerned with the earliest stages of supply, which could include drawing natural resources from the earth. Production transforms those resources into semifinished and finished goods via conversion, manufacture, or assembly. For most of the companies surveyed, the products then pass through necessary channels of distribution, often including warehousing. After some form of storage and delivery, the goods arrive at a retail outlet, and the cycle ends with consumption and recycling by the consumer. Such is the nature of the supply chain process to be considered. The organizations studied have endeavored to simplify, reengineer, and redefine their supply chains to gain market share, a sustainable competitive advantage, and ever-increasing shareholder value. Their supply chain processes will most likely never become "optimal" but will certainly continue to evolve in that direction.

As our research and direct consultation continued, the path led from a manufacturing supply chain scenario to a service environment. During the past four years, companies we studied have included financial organizations, telecommunication firms, healthcare providers, and utilities. Our analysis now extends to Allegheny Energy System, Bell Canada, Southwestern Bell, Henry Ford Healthcare, Detroit Edison, and First Chicago Bank. These service organizations have discovered that delivery to the ultimate consumer depends on—and influences—their supply chain efficiency as much as the conversion of raw materials into finished goods does for a manufacturing company. Just as Whirlpool must discover how to acquire the materials to make a customized refrigerator and deliver it quickly at the most economical cost, so a healthcare provider must learn the best way to make hospital care available for specific patients, at competitive rates.

Following deregulation, utilities have found themselves under pressure for increased efficiency. Leaders rush to consolidate geographical positions, all the while learning that delivering gas, electricity, water, and power to customers must be executed in the most effective and most efficient manner possible. If not, markets will be lost to an army of newcomers who are prepared to satisfy large users directly through a consolidated package of services that could include design, construction, and start-up services and the necessary energy sources. Utilities are scrambling to create the same kind of efficient supply chain networks that manufacturers have been developing and refining for almost a decade.

It is now apparent that the supply chain is the main artery of all businesses. As the army of logistics practitioners grows, almost exponentially, firms are throwing their best resources at whatever they call their "supply chains" in a sometimes desperate attempt to gain a lead. Hardly any firm today lacks a supply chain management department or equivalent function. Unfortunately, however, much of this effort is not effectively directed or fully understood. The result is a growing gap between the firms that truly understand and implement the concepts of effective, forward-looking supply chain management and those that simply follow a trend. Measurements of progress, most of which will be presented in this book, show a one- to two-year advantage opening between the leaders and followers. The supply chain improvement efforts will invariably produce winners and pretenders, and this distinction will strongly influence which companies acquire other companies and which ones are acquired.

These observations and experiences have led to the identification of a supply chain progress continuum, from beginning efforts to a position of global advantage. Such a progress analysis will help those interested in pursuing supply chain management to its optimal level. Significant help was offered in this analysis by individuals engaged in supply chain management, and one result has been the identification of "best practices" by the leading practitioners. As the concept grew in importance and success, so did the number of people who have acquired titles indicating direct management responsibility over the supply chain. It has been my good fortune to work with many of these people and to influence and participate in shaping their organizations and processes. This book describes the construction and evolution of a supply chain system aimed at securing a long-term market advantage and significantly increasing shareholder value.

Anyone concerned with the process of helping an organization optimize its supply chain and increase shareholder return will benefit from reading this book. Such a process succeeds only when ultimate consumers are satisfied by the network of linked firms that supply the means of satisfaction. This book builds on concepts presented in *Supply Chain Optimization,* published by Berrett-Koehler in 1996.

▶ Contents

The book begins with a brief summary of events that have made supply chain management such a timely issue and reviews some of the early results of improvement efforts, both positive and negative. I then present the various levels of accomplishment that separate the successful firms from the "wannabes." I also describe the higher levels of accomplishment that result from establishing the enabling external alliances necessary for achieving network excellence. The book will help an organization find its position on the scale of supply chain excellence. The ultimate purposes of this book are to describe supply chain management as an evolutionary process, show why only a few firms have achieved the highest status, and determine what it takes to reach advanced levels.

I include action studies in most chapters to illustrate how firms around the world have tried and are trying to attain supply chain excellence. Some companies have understood what is needed to transcend myopic, inward-looking thinking that may result in a great performance by internal standards but often misses the mark in the increasingly important global marketplace. As companies strive for the highest levels of supply chain performance, I discuss what works, what does not, and why.

▶ Acknowledgments

The individuals who were most helpful in contributing to this study are cited as case studies and action stories are presented. Special recognition must be given to Ralph Drayer of Procter & Gamble, a pioneer in the field; Don Bowersox of Michigan State University, who saw the critical importance of logistics early; Jim Morehouse of A. T. Kearney, who encouraged me to practice supply chain consulting to help other firms; Terry Ennis of Du Pont, who shared his models;

Bill Houser, who has always influenced my thinking and concepts; and Bill Read of Computer Sciences Corporation (CSC), who built a consulting practice around the leading supply chain concepts. Special thanks go to Trisha Tinney for her editorial work, to Deb Hageman for her tireless effort at creating the many versions of the product, and to Tod Roberts of Roberts Communications for his editorial advice and corrections to the final draft.

Valuable editorial comment that brought the final version to its publishable stage came particularly from Stanley Bass (who has helped in the past), Dr. John Mentzer (University of Tennessee), John Mariotti, and Catherine Dain. Helpful advice was given by many associates at CSC, especially Mike Bauer, Brad Scheller, Dave Durtsche, Rob Guzak, and Jim Gardner.

Evanston, Illinois   Charles C. Poirier
October 1998

To my family

 *Chapter 1*

Early Efforts, Mixed Results

Supply chain management has emerged as one of the most powerful business improvement tools available today. Suppliers, manufacturers, distributors, retailers, and a host of service organizations have discovered that they must either transform their operations and tactics or be beaten by competitors with more innovative and aggressive supply networks. Much effort has been expended on supply chain improvement over the past decade, when the practices were described under such labels as partnering, logistics reengineering, process redesign, or distribution-channel improvement. These efforts led to an evolution that begins with early attempts to reduce costs through improvement of purchasing, logistics, and distribution functions and progresses to advanced stages in which alliances with key partners and extensive use of interactive technology become the secrets to success.

Early efforts concentrated on improving only the internal efficiency of an individual firm or a single constituent in the supply network.

1

In today's businesses, organizations have formed networks for sourcing raw materials, manufacturing products or creating services, storing and distributing the goods, and ultimately delivering the products and services to customers and consumers. The name for this effort is *supply chain management,* and the focus is moving externally as well as internally. Early efforts concentrated on improving only the internal efficiency of an individual firm or a single constituent in the supply network. Leaders today seek ways to change, redesign, and reengineer the entire network. The latest technology is used to direct the effort toward specific markets and customer segments. Product and service innovation across the linked organizations are among the new driving forces. The emphasis is on satisfying the ultimate consumer.

Advanced supply chain management concepts are now coming into focus, but cultural pitfalls in many firms limit the acceptance of external help and the trust of partners necessary in supply chain systems. Companies must not only understand the principles behind advanced techniques but also learn the value of cooperation, redirect the internal competition for every dollar of investment toward network improvement, and solicit the help of willing partners interested in building the dominant supply chain in a particular industry. Most important, firms must learn how to balance stakeholder interests in the short term as a means of maximizing shareholder value in the long term. These will be hard lessons to learn.

As a result of the connection between the chains of supply and demand, supply chain management attracts the attention of leading firms. These companies see the value of integrating systems and supply chain operations across the full range of component functions. Business strategies are becoming intrinsically connected with supply chain and information strategies. The leaders are using advanced data systems and supply chain management techniques as a means of harmonizing organizational efforts and achieving very ambitious long-term strategic initiatives. Globalization is entering the picture in a dramatic fashion as the leading companies are forging future supply-and-demand networks that circle the globe with an integrated delivery system, appearing seamless to the final consumer.

Outsourcing supply functions to appropriate noncore outside service providers is a feature of the best of these networks, as firms learn that they cannot be all things to all customers and can benefit by concentrating on core competencies. Electronic commerce is becoming increasingly important as an enabler of sourcing and marketing through Internet capabilities, which are expanding exponentially and appealing to a whole new generation of consumers. As the new models are created, one thing is clear: the leaders are progressing more rapidly than the followers.

Retailing giant Wal-Mart has been working for over two years with Warner-Lambert to improve the accuracy of sales forecasts through collaboration over an Internet connection. Forecasts delivered through this system factor in geographical and seasonal market trends and predicted store demands. During pilot testing for Listerine products, product cycle time was reduced to six weeks from twelve. In an advanced effort, Wal-Mart's experiences with Procter & Gamble have forged the leading-edge practices for fulfilling orders directly against what has been sold by individual stores as those firms continue to take experiences to the next logical level of cooperation and reduce the cycle time from order to delivery from weeks to days.

Heineken Beer distributors input actual depletion figures and replenishment orders to the Dutch-based brewer through their linked Web pages. This interactive planning system then generates time-phased orders based on actual pull-through consumption, not anticipated demand. Distributors are then able to modify plans based on local conditions or marketing changes. These revised plans are available on a real-time basis to the European brewery, which adjusts brewing and supply schedules. Lead times have been reduced from the traditional ten to twelve weeks to four to six. In an industry focused on product freshness, this time savings enhances an already enviable market position.

some examples of success of good mgmt.

Advanced supply chain management is a practice used by leading companies to improve a total system of supply, linked directly to current demands in chosen markets, so that efficiency savings are accrued and shared across the network. The progress toward the highest stages of excellence occurs through four levels described in this book. Some companies progress faster than others, of course, and some remain stuck at Level I. In fact, the nature and speed of progress are the primary ways to distinguish the leaders from the followers.

▶ Uneven Gains

Preliminary results from supply chain improvement initiatives have been mixed. Most firms have identified and benefited from quick-hit gains and increased profits. Supply costs have been reduced to some degree through concerted improvements in the purchasing function. Inventories have been either cut or moved upstream in the supply chain, and warehousing and transportation costs have usually been reduced. Companies have applied information technology to gain an advantage over slower-reacting networks. Any software vendor offering a package that appeared to be helpful received attention from these early Level I implementers. Despite many false steps, key measurement improvements approaching 7 to 8 percent annually have been reported by companies pursuing early efforts at supply chain improvement.

A few lessons stand out in the early results. No firm as an individual entity can "shrink its way" to greatness. It must cooperate with valued suppliers and distributors. It must focus on specific markets, customers, and consumers. It must operate in an environment that is completely transparent to all constituents in the supply chain so that each player can see what moves to the customer when and can identify sources of potential savings. The barriers that inhibit the sharing of vital information—barriers that drive costs up and service down—must be exposed and overcome as a new culture is built. Shared thinking and commitment must replace fear, distrust, and arrogance if a company expects to create and maintain an efficient supply chain that dominates its markets.

Shared thinking and commitment must replace fear, distrust, and arrogance if a company expects to create and maintain an efficient supply chain that dominates its markets.

The leaders can point to dramatic double-digit percentage improvements as the result of more effective and value-adding processes. Purchasing departments have formed partnerships with selected suppliers to find extra savings that were previously hidden. The leaders have stopped inventories from moving upstream in the supply chain and have in fact eliminated inventories not linked directly with demand. Warehousing, distribution, and transportation functions have been synchronized to eliminate costs. Cycle times have been reduced to once unthinkably low levels.

Although most companies still refuse to share vital information and still lack mutually beneficial deployment of electronic data interchange, innovative leaders in some industries are working with suppliers, distributors, and customers to get products and services to the right consumers more quickly and at less cost through the use of linked information networks. Databases are mined not only to get information but also to contain costs and generate profitable revenues. The leaders use information technology to develop advanced electronic linkages and alliances with other organizations to help implement integrated supply chains in selected markets and customer segments. Software has been customized to meet the needs of the full supply system. One result is that customers become pleasantly dependent on the ease of business performance through this integrated supply network, and they reward these leading companies with a more secure order flow.

For example, Procter & Gamble now participates in a network moving the company's very familiar line of consumer products through Wal-Mart outlets. In such a network, P&G knows by cash register and by store what products have passed through the system during the day. This network is linked by satellite communications on a real-time basis. With actual point-of-sale information and a supporting system of supply designed for efficiency and cost control, products are replenished to meet current demand and minimize stockouts while maintaining industry-leading low inventories. Procter & Gamble possesses one of the most advanced leading-edge networks.

While the leaders were approaching advanced levels of supply chain excellence, other firms struggled to achieve similar results. The published case studies began to show the way, but a missing factor was plaguing the less successful organizations. It is now clear that failure developed in two key areas: a lack of trust and sincere effort among necessary participants in the chain and a myopic view focused solely on internal gains.

Progress in developing trust was neither made nor sustained because the firms that were engaged in supply chain redesign did not grasp the need for sharing the savings with the organizations that helped improve the system. Along the way, such firms also failed to develop cross-organizational trust, which is now recognized as a crucial success factor. In these early efforts, some firms sought an advantage at the expense of suppliers by leveraging their position with those firms and pocketing all the savings, which were eventually given away to equally hungry customers. It became a zero-sum game, and that is a prescription for failure.

Some firms took another path and created competitively advantaged supply chains by developing trust with a select group of suppliers, distributors, and customers. Within these networks, data and savings were shared, confidentiality was secured, and systems were interconnected to ensure that the knowledge could be transferred quickly and safely. The sharing of previously sacrosanct information among the former loosely related constituents resulted in reduced cycle times because this new approach allowed inventories to be placed at the point of need and distribution to be performed by whichever supply chain participant could do it most efficiently.

Unless a company shares the savings gained from improved supply chain management, the persons who enabled the savings will be less likely to provide more improvement ideas in the future. As some companies achieved early supply chain improvements, they tried to find as much savings as possible as quickly as possible so that they could cut manufacturing costs and retail prices. In the process, these organizations learned that the only beneficiaries were the retailer and the ultimate consumers. Profit margins stayed the same, and the flow of innovative suggestions slowed. By contrast, leaders focus on creating profitable revenue growth through the building of alliances with constituents across the entire supply chain, and they share the gains realized through greater efficiency. Such firms are now linked interactively with their supply chain partners in delivering fairly priced products and services to delighted consumers. In the process, they are creating above-average returns on their investments, as well as higher shareholder value.

Some firms reach a point where they become arrogant regarding their progress and the degree to which internal performance is improved. In many cases the pride in accomplishment may be justified, but the self-congratulation escalates to the point where market advantage is put at risk. These firms become very skilled at cutting costs and increasing organizational efficiency, only to realize that they are still going to market with products that are no longer in demand among consumers. Leading companies realize that internal operational excellence must be balanced with external supply network efficiency, the ultimate objective of which is to please the final consumer.

The leaders began their journey by breaking down the traditional internal barriers to progress by encouraging (or, when necessary, forcing) internal functional departments to cooperate in providing excellent customer service and pleasing the final consumer. Supply chain improvement initiatives proved to be an excellent cross-functional discipline that required the various internal groups to put aside their turf issues and focus on building an advantaged distribution system. Many companies succeeded in improving cooperation among internal functions and gaining significant operational benefits. However, the leaders went on to establish external partnerships with suppliers and distributors. Such partnering resulted in new ways of supplying products and services to the customers along the chain, down to the ultimate consumers. Most of these firms also developed innovative applications to take advantage of the burgeoning databases created through partnering relationships. These vaults of knowledge were full of demand information that could be linked across the entire supply network, allowing traditional push systems to be transformed into a smooth-flowing network driven by actual consumer demand.

In short, the new supply chain game is becoming a competition between effective supply networks rather than individual corporations, and the gap between the leaders and followers is growing rapidly.

Advanced supply networks allow appropriate products and services to be pulled from the system in the most effective and optimized manner possible with current technology. In the best cases, the latest and most appropriate information technology is applied to solidify the newly established competitive advantage. In short, the new supply chain game is becoming a competition between effective supply networks rather than individual corporations, and the gap between the leaders and followers is growing rapidly.

▶ A Helpful Model

The way organizations plan their routes and conduct successful journeys toward supply chain excellence is shown in Exhibit 1.1. This model begins with the delivery of raw material from a supplier to a manufacturer or converter. The supply might consist of grain, sweeteners, fruit, vegetables, and packaging to a food processor; metal, plastics, windows, moldings, and subassemblies to an automobile manufacturer; or chemicals, fibers, colorants, and buttons to a clothing fabricator. The manufacturer receives the materials via some mode of transportation (railroad car, truck, plane, or ship) and puts the material into temporary storage to await further processing.

Service industries follow a similar path, but the source of materials is different. For example, in a bank, the flow would begin with computer suppliers, furniture, business forms, and telecommunication equipment and would end in a lending institution for conversion into loan and credit applications for corporations and individuals. In a healthcare system, the flow would start with materials such as gauze, paper products, surgical instruments, and intravenous devices for patient care. A hospital would then store these materials until needed.

The supply flow often requires some type of manufacturing or conversion operation to turn the raw materials into a finished product or a deliverable service. At the completion of the conversion, the products are in the form of finished or semifinished goods, to be transported through an appropriate channel of distribution. Products as large as automobiles go by truck directly to a dealer or by railroad carriers to a staging area for delivery to area dealers. Because of the large number of smaller items being supplied in a typical chain of delivery and the range in size of retail customers, distributors are often involved. High-volume consumer products can move directly from manufacturing to a large customer in truckload quantities, but low-volume items must be gathered in bulk at a staging area by a distributor, broken down and packaged into smaller units, and transferred to local customers unable to order truckloads or large volumes of the item. A pallet load of paper towels might make sense for some

EXHIBIT 1.1
Supply Chain Management: Areas of Opportunity

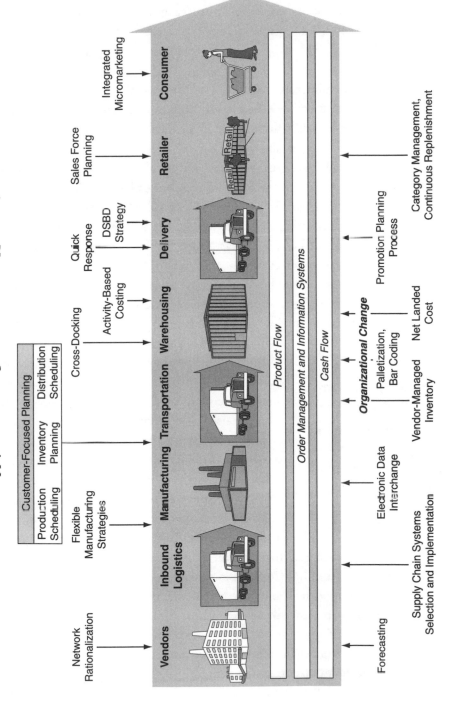

retailers and could be direct-shipped, but a pallet load of a particular food seasoning would be a multiyear supply for a small specialty food retailer. The model therefore includes warehouses or distribution centers, where appropriate, for completing the delivery of goods and services.

The customer in the model is some type of retailer or institution that sells and delivers the final product and service to the ultimate consumer, generally through a store or local facility. For food delivery, a grocery store or chain such as Kroger, Safeway, or Food Lion would be an appropriate customer. For automobiles, it would be a local dealership or one of the growing number of large multibrand organizations. For clothing, a department store like Dayton Hudson, Macy's, or Bloomingdale's is the traditional retail outlet, but specialty chains like The Gap, Victoria's Secret, or The Limited could be the preferred customer. A healthcare system like Columbia or an individual hospital could be the targeted customer for a supplier of medicine, pharmaceuticals, or patient care products.

In all cases, the flow of the product or service moves toward the ultimate consumer, who purchases the goods and services for personal reasons. Simply put, the satisfaction of the individual consumer should drive a company to analyze, manage, and improve its supply chain continuously. The buying options are currently so large and the loyalties so weak that shifts in consumption patterns can be swift and deadly. Whether the chain is for products or services, the flow may appear to be from left to right, and most improvement efforts have been conducted in that direction. In reality, however, an analysis of the chain should focus on the finish line (demand), not the starting point (supply). Companies that believe that the primary objective of supply chain improvements is to improve internal efficiency rather than to serve ultimate consumers more effectively are doomed to fail in today's competitive environment.

In reality, however, an analysis of the chain should focus on the finish line (demand), not the starting point (supply).

The supply chain model in Exhibit 1.1 shows several early effort improvement opportunities that companies have pursued to create more efficient supply chains and gain cost savings. Most organizations began by rationalizing the supply network. One early effort was to reduce the number of suppliers, originally to improve consistency in the quality of incoming materials. It was assumed that this action would result in both better quality and lower cost. When this effort revealed weaknesses in some suppliers, the next step was to rationalize (reduce the size of) the supplier base. Suppliers who survived this process gained large-volume positions in exchange for cost concessions.

Some companies pursued the benefits of flexible manufacturing systems and focused on planning and scheduling as two key ingredients that would dramatically reduce inventory, fabrication, and conversion costs. This effort went by many names, but "customer-focused planning" captures the basic concept. Using some type of demand information, companies established systems that could more efficiently manage the process of acquiring the right raw materials, having the necessary machine time and human resources available, and scheduling output to meet demand without excess stores and inventories. Material resource planning (MRP) was the earliest effort, followed by MRP II. This methodology evolved into distribution resource planning (DRP) and eventually enterprise resource planning (ERP) as the level of sophistication and complexity of the software increased. The systems application process (SAP), which originated in Germany, has become the favorite of firms seeking the ultimate in manufacturing control processing.

Firms soon discovered that forecasting was going to be (and continues to be) a controlling factor in the efficiency of these systems. The amount of inventory and safety stocks required to maintain high order-fill rates and the reliability of manufacturing schedules are directly related to the accuracy of the data predicting what the supply system will require by customer and location. Most of the early work in this area was fruitless because it was too difficult to implement the discipline required to determine reliable input on demand, on the part of both buyers and sellers. In spite of growing collections of historical data, better techniques at predicting demand and seasonal shifts, and closer communications with customers, most forecasters relied on intuition and last year's results. Typical forecast accuracy was measured in the neighborhood of 40 percent.

In actual practice, most firms gave up on sophisticated planning techniques and worked off the projected business plans, which called for annual increases in volume regardless of market conditions. The numbers used to establish financial targets were used as often as other data to determine monthly sales forecasts. Supply chain systems were then selected and attempts were made at implementing delivery to these spurious and often fictitious projections of consumer need. The result was a hodgepodge of planning and scheduling that was constantly subjected to manual overrides for meeting actual consumer demand.

Electronic data interchange (EDI) looked like the possible panacea. Retailers rushed to install electronic equipment to pick up cash register information that would measure actual consumption. The theory was that these data could be fed back into the supply network and replenishment would flow in synchronization with actual consumption. This concept proved generally unsuccessful because of errors by the clerks doing the entry, as well as the lack of universal coding systems. EDI was also expected to eliminate the glaciers of paper flowing between most linked constituents in the supply chain. Purchase orders were to move electronically, acknowledgments were to be eliminated as the accuracy of the data was increased, and payment was to be in the form of electronically transferred funds.

Some of these visions were achieved, and a few leaders pressed forward to establish virtual inventories so that materials in a pipeline of supply could be checked and verified electronically in real time. Most firms at the early stages of supply chain improvement are still struggling with the implementation process. In the advanced stages, to be described later, firms that require accurate forecasts to gain any advantage from their supply chain systems focus on managing the process. These firms use techniques and software that dramatically improve accuracy, often to 80 percent or more.

Many firms concentrated their efforts farther downstream in the model when direct store delivery (DSD), vendor-managed inventory (VMI), or category management systems came into vogue. This required further attention to improving forecasts or, at the least, collaborating with suppliers and customers to determine more accurately what is needed from suppliers and what is being sold to consumers. Bar-coding the individual products, packages, and pallet loads became crucial to the success of these programs and often stalled because of a lack of standards or agreeable formats between parties. Efficient consumer response (ECR) became a driving force particularly in the food distribution arena as food retailers responded to an industry study that showed a potential savings of $30 billion through more efficient handling, storage, and delivery of products in their supply chains.

The accountants then entered the supply chain and very correctly suggested that someone take a look at activity-based costs and the net landed cost of delivering products and services. Emphasis shifted to analyzing, by market, customer, and product, whether or not a true profit was being made. In many cases, firms discovered that the cost of extra handling and servicing negated the possibility of generating a profit on certain customers or through certain product lines. Customer and product rationalization (reducing the number of customers served and the number of products being offered for sale) was pursued as a way to increase the viability and profitability of the supply network. Promotion planning and sales force planning came under scrutiny when the concept of the supply chain was expanded to include sales and after-sale service. Some companies were surprised to discover as much opportunity to reduce costs and improve efficiencies on the selling side of the chain as on the manufacturing and supply side. Later efforts focused on linking the demand chain with the supply chain in a holistic manner to achieve cost reductions throughout the entire chain.

Micromarketing became one technique to determine, by store, how the product offering should look, to maximize the use of the floor space allocated to selling. Entirely new sections or departments showed up in the retail stores, bringing goods with ethnic, age, or gender appeal to designated micromarkets. Product offerings by stock-keeping unit (SKU) were both reduced and enlarged to match the actual buying patterns being documented by the cash registers recording consumption. Such activities were driving forces behind quick response (QR) and the shortest possible cycle time.

No single firm chased all of these initiatives (and others not listed in Exhibit 1.1), but a few organizations pooled their efforts into a network of supply to realize the benefits that could come from their implementation. In all cases, improved order management and information systems were central to the success of the efforts. The key was to capture the flow of data forward and backward across the chain so that a firm could determine and react to actual consumer buying behavior. Cash flow increased for firms finding the right answers because of significant reductions in inventories and faster billing and payment.

▶ Early Results

The earliest supply chain improvement efforts validated the concept that concerted, integrated reforms across a full delivery system could yield substantial benefits. Where those improvements were found varied by organization and type of product or service, but a pattern quickly developed.

The earliest supply chain improvement efforts validated the concept that concerted, integrated reforms across a full delivery system could yield substantial benefits.

Attention to supply chain activities initially led to improvements in internal functions such as order entry and fulfillment, credit application, planning and scheduling, logistics, and warehousing and distribution. The initial efforts typically included a rudimentary process mapping, displaying the flow of primary products and services to a few key market segments and customers. General Electric was in the forefront of this technique. Project teams were formed to develop potentially high-payback initiatives that would yield savings to fund future efforts.

Early initiatives invariably included a heavy emphasis on logistics and reducing freight and distribution costs. Such efforts were strongly aided by the Council of Logistics Management, a forum for sharing information on improvement concepts and techniques. The effort then typically expanded to warehouse costs, the consolidation of facilities, and the introduction of third-party organizations to perform some or all of the logistical functions. Trucking firms formed new organizations to provide total delivery systems.

The effort quickly expanded to purchasing, followed by supply sourcing (the process of buying and having products and services delivered to a firm), for conversion into goods delivered to a customer. Firms realized that 50 to 70 percent of their costs could be related to purchasing. Exhibit 1.2 illustrates the range of expenditures, as a percentage of the sales dollar, for a large sample of manufacturing organizations. Although cost could be reduced in almost every category, most paled in comparison to purchasing. Dramatic results were recorded as organizations focused some of their best talent on this highest-cost segment. Teams worked with the supply base to reduce the number of suppliers and found ways to leverage a larger position in exchange for pricing and servicing concessions.

Unfortunately, most of these early savings were quickly passed on to the retailer or end user in an effort to gain a larger volume position

EXHIBIT 1.2

Expenditure Levels: Critical Areas for Cost Reduction
and Process Improvement

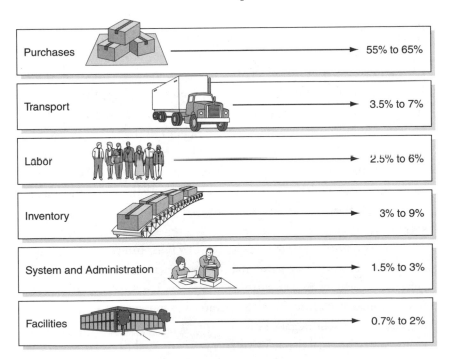

Purchases	55% to 65%
Transport	3.5% to 7%
Labor	2.5% to 6%
Inventory	3% to 9%
System and Administration	1.5% to 3%
Facilities	0.7% to 2%

near the back of the supply chain. The retailer was equally quick to pass the savings on to the consumer, and the net effect was a loss of savings in the delivering network of supply. What should have been impressive gains in earnings per share for the manufacturers and retailers vaporized as the efforts of purchasing agents, buyers, planners, schedulers, operators, engineers, designers, and a host of logistics and delivery personnel were aggregated into supply chain savings that became bargaining chips for volume increases.

Such actions slowed down the flow of innovative ideas, and most supply chains reached a state of equilibrium as upstream suppliers and manufacturers began to withhold from the downstream customers ideas and actions that would yield further savings. Attention shifted to improvement in internal mechanisms as a source of savings. In an unfortunate change of circumstances, the rhetoric continued focusing on the "supply chain improvements" as a means of satisfying customers, but the capital funds were channeled to projects to increase operational efficiency. The emphasis shifted from satisfying the customer to cutting costs.

▶ Focus on Internal Operations

Continued efforts at supply chain improvement were constrained to finding internal savings, the benefits of which were kept from downstream customers. Not surprisingly, companies next concentrated on how to deal with the lack of internal cooperation that inhibited effective supply chain processing. Jack Welch, CEO of General Electric, expressed this concern in a speech he gave in March 1994: "GE needs to be a company without boundaries. . . . We will view turfism as a major internal disease to be treated as severely as passing on company secrets."

Welch's comment points to the issue of poor internal partnering; he rightly identified departmental turf battles as a serious obstacle to genuine reform. A movement to remove these internal barriers and to encourage cross-functional cooperation as a means of better meeting customer needs began. However, firms ran into opposition from almost every internal department and were stymied in creating a truly efficient supply chain that would meet both internal and external needs.

Engineering created designs that were difficult to manufacture. In turn, manufacturing made products that marketing did not want to sell, and sales brought in orders that languished because they were "manufacturing unfriendly." Well-meaning employees were very reluctant to work effectively together with other departments inside the firm for the overall benefit of the firm. It was much easier to place blame for failure in the chain on another function than to cooperate in making the chain error-free. Departmental or functional excellence was considered much more important than delivering the right products and services to the final consumer in the most efficient manner. Breaking down these internal barriers became a major challenge because change-resistant corporate bureaucracies flourished inside business organizations.

production challenges.

When cross-functional cooperation became a targeted improvement issue, "supply chain teams" came into vogue. Managers were urged by senior executives to find opportunities for intra- and interdepartmental cooperation. This most difficult of supply chain management challenges still stymies many organizations, but some found a way to remove internal turf barriers and institute genuine teamwork among formerly competing functions. Indeed, the use of effective teams can overcome significant competitive disadvantages in scale and reach. One effective tool in breaking down these barriers was the extensive use of hourly workers in finding solutions to long-standing manufacturing and delivery problems.

> *Indeed, the use of effective teams can overcome significant competitive disadvantages in scale and reach.*

An important lesson must be passed on here. It is not enough to find and document the potential savings that may be realized by supply chain improvements. In addition, the people given responsibility for implementing improvements must have a sincere desire to implement them. I worked with one large manufacturer of recreational products to document potential savings from changes in sourcing ranging from $30 to $50 million annually. The teams created to find those savings did everything possible to validate the savings, including conducting some of the preliminary negotiations in test categories with the help of current buyers. After the action plan was completed, enthusiasm for the project languished. Neither implementation nor potential savings ever happened.

A later analysis showed that the buyers simply refused to change their existing supply base. A consistent flow of meaningless rhetoric was delivered in an attempt to get the leaders to reduce the pressure to eliminate the current, higher-cost suppliers. The buyers, when confronted with evidence of the validated lower costs, ignored the better quotations, claiming that the new sources would not match the service levels known in the past. When pilot tests showed superior levels of service, the buyers still refused to make the changes, apparently because of an unwillingness to give up long-standing personal relationships with suppliers.

Another unfortunate experience occurred, from a reverse perspective, with a selling organization. In this case, the national account sales organization found an opportunity with one of the firm's largest customers, entering into a single-sourcing arrangement on the supply of packaging. The customer invited several national suppliers to participate, with the caveat that one source had to supply across all receiving locations with no deterioration in quality or service. Working with the proposing team, efforts were expended to get all of the local supplying plant managers involved because customer sites required shipments from a multitude of plants. Most of the plant managers cooperated earnestly. Two of the managers were reluctant participants, owing, as a later analysis showed, to personal jealousy toward members of the national account selling team. Following the award of the contract by the customer, these managers let it be known at their plant sites that the new business would receive second priority to locally sold accounts. The results were disastrous. Service levels and quality deteriorated at the two plants, and this situation alone caused the cancellation of the contract. Dismissing the plant managers did nothing to assuage the customer. The damage had been done.

Early efforts at supply chain optimization proved that the enemy is typically within the organization. Supply chain improvement efforts, by their nature, have to cross division, department, function, location, and turf boundaries. The people within those boundaries will initially endorse any effort designed to significantly improve processes, reduce operating costs, increase revenues, and bring the firm into the modern era. Much of that endorsement is cosmetic and must be watched closely. There is far greater concern in the beginning of a supply chain improvement effort about maintaining the status quo than in making necessary changes. This is an unfortunate fact of life in business organizations. A simple but hard-learned lesson may apply here: begin with a small project to prove the concepts and complications, and develop answers before proceeding to larger and more complex opportunities. Start with a project you know will be successful.

▶ Inventory: A New Hot Topic

In organizations achieving new levels of internal cooperation, additional areas of improvement were considered. When teams focused on what was really in the supply pipelines, inventory became a favorite target. The findings were often shocking—hidden inventories were discovered to be equal to recorded inventories, due especially to a lack of trust in the internal systems providing and recording the flow of needed materials and finished goods. The hidden category included large quantities of damaged or obsolete products and supplies that were still being stored somewhere in the organization, mainly because managers refused to take the necessary write-off costs. This category also included materials squirreled away in secret areas, for what was believed to be emergency situations. In one example, a hospital found stores of critical material hidden in acoustic panels in the ceiling by nurses convinced that the supply network could not be trusted.

The visible, or recorded, category came under close scrutiny to decide whether it was the right inventory matched to current demand, whether it could be pushed back to a supplier, and whether features of consignment could be attached. Too often, the inventory was found to contain superfluous product that was no longer in demand. Obsolete and damaged parts were brought to light. The expression "aged inventories" took on new meaning. Parts were unearthed, being held for machines that were no longer at the factory. Perishable goods were found that were beyond their shelf life. The game became how to deal with these revelations and how to get another party to take inventory the firm wanted to get off the books. In one classic example, a firm sent fifty-three truckloads of inventory back to the supplier just before a year-end physical accounting was to be taken.

Some firms recorded dramatic reductions as they applied a just-in-time (JIT) approach and slashed inventories to what was needed to support the current, real flow of product to customers. The measurement of inventory turns (annual sales divided by average inventory) became a standard way to determine progress. Many early results revealed turns as low as once or twice per year. Such measures proved that a significant amount of inventory was sitting around for an entire year waiting to be passed to an actual consumer. Damage to such goods, failure to find stocks kept in storage for long periods, and simple duplication of orders led to an incredible amount of waste. Inventory continues to be a major area of opportunity as firms seek savings in a supply chain.

▶ Another Opportunity Area: Human Error

Order entry and fulfillment followed next when firms discovered an army of clerical personnel at work cleaning up errors and mistakes made on incoming orders. Reconciling the mistakes occurring in supply chain processing created additional work for those doing nothing more than covering other people's lack of discipline. Some organizations found errors in pricing alone that were worth several points of net profit. Mistakes were found in virtually every hand-off across a chain of supply. Paperwork to record the transactions not only abounded but proliferated for checking and counterchecking the poor processing. After the mess was cleaned up, technology was often applied to automate the new processes and keep errors to a minimum.

Reconciling the mistakes occurring in supply chain processing created additional work for those doing nothing more than covering other people's lack of discipline.

For example, a pasta manufacturer took the time to determine how orders were actually processed. For this specific firm, orders came from three sources: direct sales representatives, agents, and brokers. Territory was divided among these sources to minimize conflicts and to ensure coverage of all possible customers. A price list was developed once a year and set in place for all products. Discount schedules were also negotiated with the agents and brokers, based on past performance and volume with customers. However, this seemingly simple process was full of complications.

The first problem was that no discipline was applied in adhering to the negotiated discounts. When an agent or broker found an attractive piece of business, a price deemed necessary to secure the business was given to the customer and entered into order fulfillment with the pasta manufacturer. The order entry department accepted all orders and passed them to the planning department. Billing was based on the negotiated process, and invoices were issued at the designated prices, followed then by a flurry of activity when both parties entered into reconciliation. What happened next could have been predicted. A clerk was placed into negotiation with a seasoned broker, sales agent, or representative who had a large piece of business in hand. It was no contest—the lower price prevailed, regardless of negotiation. Not only was the firm wasting its time on the group of clerks fighting with agents and brokers, but it was also missing the extra points of discount given without approval to obtain the business.

The second problem was that in spite of the personal computers in the hands of the sales reps, agents, and brokers, very few were capable of using the computers effectively. Rather than entering orders as prescribed, orders were being sent in that were illegible, incomplete, and lacking in accurate delivery information. By enforcing an automated system, including fail-safe techniques that refused the order unless it was complete, accurate, and correctly priced, this firm picked up 3 percent net profit in the first year.

▶ Conclusion: Supply Chain Improvements Work

Early results generally left many organizations satisfied that supply chain improvement efforts were worth the investment, yet they rested on their laurels. A few leaders decided that there would be at least as great a benefit if the effort were extended cautiously beyond the internal walls, with firms they could trust. These leaders began a concerted effort to think outside of the narrow walls that limit innovation and provide only incremental results. They looked for partnering opportunities with a very select group of suppliers, distributors, and customers in order for the benefits to be extended and enlarged. Leaders such as Procter & Gamble and Wal-Mart have created a new model for supply chain interaction, in which optimization is approached. Their networking set a standard that put them a year or two ahead of their competition.

For most firms, implementation of internal improvement opportunities will still yield large benefits, even if the companies have failed to keep up with the leaders. Projects can focus on areas where there is now ample "best practice" data to guide the initiatives. Logistics offers particularly rich improvement opportunities, followed by sourcing, planning, inventory management, new product introduction, and order fulfillment. For those in search of even more opportunities, advanced supply chain management is of great interest.

 *Chapter 2*

Success on Progressive Levels

Those who pursue supply chain improvement seek the secret solutions that can push their organization to the head of the class. However, there are no easy answers. The road to a leading-edge position requires focus, dedication, creativity, and hard work. Exhibit 2.1 is a compact illustration of the four levels through which a firm evolves to achieve advanced stages of supply chain management and to realize the rewards that result from a drive for

> *A firm that believes it can jump to the highest level is going to find the effort fruitless.*

optimization. Based on the experience of many companies to date, there is no way to avoid moving through these levels of progression. A firm that believes it can jump to the highest level is going to find the effort fruitless. A firm in the first level that wishes to be at the fourth level must develop a strategy for rapid movement through the intermediate levels.

The first two levels, labeled "Internal," occur within the organization and represent the position of most

EXHIBIT 2.1
Levels of Supply Chain Optimization

	Internal		External	
	Sourcing and Logistics I	**Internal Excellence II**	**Network Construction III**	**Industry Leadership IV**
Driver	VP sourcing (under pressure)	CIO/supply chain leader	Business unit leaders	Management team
Benefits	Leveraged savings	Prioritized improvements across network	Best partner performance	Network advantage, profitable revenue
Focus	Inventory, logistics, freight, order fulfillment	Process redesign, system improvement	Forecasting, planning, customer services, interenterprise	Consumer, network
Tools	Teaming, functional excellence	Benchmarks, best practice, activity-based costing	Metrics, database mining, electronic commerce	Intranet, Internet, virtual information systems
Action Area	Midlevel organization	Expanded levels	Total organization	Full enterprise
Guidance	Cost data, success funding	Process mapping	Advanced cost models, differentiating processes	Demand-supply linkage
Model	None	Supply chain—intraenterprise	Interenterprise	Global market
Alliances	Supplier consolidation	Best partner	Formal alliances	Joint ventures
Training	Team	Leadership	Partnering	Network processing

business organizations seeking improvements in their supply chains. Eighty percent of the businesses studied are somewhere in this first half of the illustration. The last two levels, labeled "External," occur when the business joins forces with external firms to seek network savings. Few organizations have reached these latter levels, where the true leaders are making the most progress. Arrayed along the vertical axis of the table are key elements in supply chain management that will be used to describe the evolution.

Beginning at the upper left-hand side of the table, the *driver*, or typical champion who promotes the necessary change process in Level I, can be a senior manager or department director who wants or is designated to institute a change process. The emphasis generally begins with encouragement or a dictum from a CEO but quickly gravitates to the vice presidential level or lower. The purpose could be to achieve a substantial gain in cost containment, to organize a concerted improvement effort, or to reengineer a process that has risen dramatically in cost. These champions then select team leaders from two sources: volunteers and conscripts.

When mergers occur, it is not unusual for a supply chain initiative to be instigated for assistance with the transformation process. A number of managers and team leaders are usually recruited in such a situation. Their purpose is to design and implement the processes that will help guide the combined organizations. In this way, the merger moves more smoothly and important areas of the business process are improved. When Duquesne Light Company agreed to merge with Allegheny Power to form Allegheny Energy Company, serving customers in western Pennsylvania, several teams were immediately formed to help with the transition. One was designated as the supply chain design team, while others focused on improving functional areas. Membership from both organizations and designated process champions were keys to success with all teams.

Experience indicates that responsibility may start with a variety of functional senior executives, but it soon ends with a senior procurement manager, such as the vice president of purchasing or sourcing. That is not always the case, but it does illustrate the process typical in Level I. This assignment occurs because of the

Most members in the purchasing function in large corporations are familiar with the pressures placed on wringing concessions from suppliers in the early phases of supply chain improvements and partnering activities.

large percentage of costs normally controlled by activities in this sector, the natural tendency to put intense emphasis on cutting the costs of purchased goods and services, and the fact that it involves all facets of operations. Most members in the purchasing function in large corporations are familiar with the pressures placed on wringing concessions from suppliers in the early phases of supply chain improvements and partnering activities.

Experience to date suggests that a company should be wary of the consequences of this approach. As participants examined and altered their supply base, processes, systems, and practices to support current requirements and objectives more effectively, they also discovered some changes that might not improve their position in the marketplace. Firms became very adept, for example, at cutting costs through the leveraging of their volume and buying position with suppliers. But many also paid a price in diminished quality and service. When a supplier anxiously accepts price concessions for volume position, a red flag should be raised to determine whether this action will result in lower-quality service and supply performance.

One automobile manufacturer gained particular notoriety for forcing unwanted concessions on its supply base, to the point of disregarding contracts and long-term supply agreements. Those efforts were followed by plant shutdowns, necessitated because vital parts were not shipped on time or because parts were inferior in quality. The lesson is obvious. If a supplying firm accepts cost transfer from a manufacturer, there is a transfer of profits as well—the buyer gains and the supplier loses. The supplier has only two choices: to recoup the lost profits through internal efficiencies or to pass back an equivalent amount of cost to the buyer. Suppliers can be very clever at the second part of the game.

A superior technique found by some organizations gave the process greater value. These organizations worked with suppliers, removing costs from the system of supply and manufacture so both parties gain an advantage and share in the additional profits generated. I will elaborate on this technique as higher levels of supply chain improvement are considered.

▶ Proof in Best Practice

The lessons learned from Level I efforts showed the way for achieving true sourcing savings. The emphasis must be on using mutual resources for mutual advantage, rather than accepting cost push-back from one company to another. A Level I organization found this to be the case when it worked with its suppliers to find major savings. Marketing Services Group (a fictitious name) bought $400 million annually of promotional materials, graphics services, and store displays. The firm then packaged these materials into sales promotion programs for a variety of consumer products firms and parallel industries. When the company began looking at savings in the supply chain, the emphasis predictably shifted to the purchasing department.

The buying staff was adequate for the traditional tasks, but an independent evaluation revealed that the staff lacked modern negotiating skills. All purchases followed a time-honored practice, insisting on three bids and selecting the lowest bidder as the supplier of choice. The buyers consistently received assurance that the supplier was selling at the lowest possible price given to any customer. Over 50 percent of the purchase orders were under $10,000, and most vendors received less than $50,000 annually, resulting in many discussions with suppliers and numerous orders. The firm understandably described its relationship with the supply base as "less than loyal."

Further investigation revealed that despite the buyers' firm conviction that they had negotiated the best possible deal, reputable suppliers showed little trust in the company. In addition, the buyers lacked confidence in the supply base and its capability to help the firm. Benchmarking comparisons, performed reluctantly, showed that prices were exceptionally high, despite the formal bidding process. Information gained from a panel of pooled customers revealed the perception that competitors were delivering superior quality. Late shipments and delayed promotions were the standard rather than the exception for Marketing Services, which relied heavily on long-term relationships rather than quality and service to secure orders from customers.

Fortunately, the results from this Level I study were successful in reversing the situation. After a careful selection process, Marketing Services sat down with the best of its suppliers and developed a win-win situation. The firm outsourced $400 million of promotion programs to two suppliers. It began the process by doing the unthinkable—turning a function over to an external firm that could accomplish the job more effectively. Supplier A supplied the basic promotional materials. Supplier B received these materials and printed most of the promotional copy. Supplier B stored, staged, kitted, and assembled the materials for appropriate promotions. Supplier B also distributed all promotional materials to the sales force or direct to the retail customers. This change forced a reorganization on the firm, but the results were dramatic. Through the elimination of clerical activities employed to cover for mistakes and shortcomings in the old system, an increased sales availability of 40 percent appeared. Outsourcing reduced operating costs by 12 percent. On-time delivery of promotional materials rose to 85 percent, from less than 60 percent. A subsequent customer survey revealed that users were highly satisfied with the new business practices.

▶ Benefits at the First Level

An early benefit of supply chain improvement efforts included project work by teams that reduced purchasing costs, inventories, logistical costs, and freight costs. As these teams were sent in search of quick opportunities, *benefits* were quickly identified and used to verify the importance of the effort. Exhibit 2.1 shows leveraged savings. Beginning efforts invariably included a trading of sales volume (the leverage) for some form of savings (the benefit).

Caution should be exercised, however, because experience has shown that some Level I savings are fictitious. If a cost is simply pushed back to an obliging supplier interested in holding an inventory (and thereby incurring the additional working capital cost) in exchange for a larger volume position, the savings within the supply system are merely apparent, not real. In the case cited, the inventory is neither reduced nor eliminated from the total supply chain. The inventory carrying cost has simply been temporarily transferred within the supply network until the obliging supplier can figure a way to regain the cost of the concessions through future pricing or reduction of quality and service. Real savings begin when the

> *Beginning efforts invariably included a trading of sales volume (the leverage) for some form of savings (the benefit).*

network completely eliminates the need for the inventory by simplifying the process or eliminating steps that require extra inventory. In these cases, the carrying cost is eliminated on the inventory no longer required to sustain delivery performance.

A large midwestern utility discovered the potential weaknesses of early results. One of its initial efforts was to cut what was considered excess inventories held for start-up applications. Transformers, cable, wire, connectors, and similar materials were held in district warehouses, allowing crews to access what they needed for project work. The buyer at the utility went to the supply base and got several distributors to accept responsibility for much of this inventory. The claimed savings was the elimination of $300 million of inventory and the carrying costs for that inventory. A later audit revealed that the distributor had accepted the inventory but was now charging an equivalent carrying charge plus an occasional special delivery charge. There were no net savings to the network of supply, and the utility's cost had actually risen.

▶ Limited Focus of First Efforts

As the *focus* is placed on specific supply chain projects such as inventory, logistics, freight, and order fulfillment, additional care must be taken to validate the assumed results. These areas were selected following purchasing because they represented large sectors of cost to most firms and were generally not being performed to leading-edge standards. Teams that went looking for opportunities to cut costs found some of the early savings mentioned. Their focus led to two approaches: either redesign or reengineer the process to become more efficient or find an external firm to which the process could be entrusted ("outsourced") in order for the firm to concentrate on core activities.

Freight was a particularly fertile area of concentration. Some firms excel at this process, while others are weak. The latter firms showed an early inclination to look at outsourcing. Experienced transportation companies know about tractors and trailers, shipments, routes, drivers, contract negotiating, terminal storage and delivery, and other relevant matters. When approached by a frustrated firm considering a professional organization to take over transportation, the trucker usually responds positively. But the trucker has to make a profit on the arrangement for it to be an attractive business proposition.

Following deregulation of the industry, pricing competition increased and margins became very thin for most trucking firms. An equitable outsourcing arrangement must include the means to gain a few points of margin for both organizations, or it will be a losing situation. For the trucker, who must accept the liabilities that come with a typical Teamster contract for the drivers, there are risks associated with the new arrangement. As a solution, the trucker may assume responsibility for the outsourcing firm's fleet of tractors and trailers, including maintenance of the fleet and the contract with the drivers. There are no savings at this point, only cost transfer. The savings appear when the trucker discovers other uses for the drivers and equipment, which eventually bring incremental profits. Usually, the trucker seeks and finds back-haul opportunities to increase fleet utilization. Early efforts produced mixed results; some firms realized the extra savings and others did not.

Order fulfillment turned out to be a challenge because most of the problems in this area were internal to the organization. A total lack of discipline was the source of most problems, showing errors well beyond anything acceptable to a manufacturing environment. The problem began with order entry and continued as the orders were processed and sent to planning, manufacturing, and delivery. Manual overrides were constantly necessary because of sloppy entry, omitted data, improper codes, erroneous pricing, and other mistakes. Often schedules went to the shop floors based on extremely poor order forecasts and incorrect shipping information. Distribution of blame was often more important to internal investigators in this area than making beneficial changes. When companies found solutions, they often rushed to eliminate people in this process. Labor savings often resulted as errors were eliminated, processes were simplified, and automated systems were created and implemented.

A cereal producer found a way to improve order fulfillment and win major rewards from its customers. This firm had annual sales of $4 billion and seven manufacturing sites. The firm completed delivery through strategically located regional distribution centers. It analyzed sales processing, credit performance, transportation costs, inventory replenishment cost, and customer service to identify several improvement opportunities in a Level I effort.

Early studies found that many employees were involved in handling the orders, reconciling the errors, making changes to meet customer demands, and getting the product through the system as "complete orders." Manual processing was more prevalent than automated techniques. Backorders were an expected part of the system, and closings were delayed because of the time required to finalize the reconciliation. Expediting and heroic customer service were the customary means of dealing with the shortcomings of the existing process. Extra personnel were clearly involved because of inefficiency.

The organization decided to form regional teams at headquarters to improve the process. It established a "leaders among peers" management system to guide the effort. Through this system, champions were selected to lead teams in analyzing work flows. For recommending streamlined activities, two caveats were important. Improvements had to result in substantially better performance and a perception of customization in the eyes of the customer. The latter objective involves an emerging concept: a supply system that the customer or final consumer perceives as a process designed to deliver a customized product or service for a particular market segment or, better, for an individual customer. Specific and often personal information is used to bring a finished product to a consumer. It may require minor modification in the manufacturing process but offers customized features (for example, motorcycle handlebars with a specific reach) for the individual consumer.

For the cereal manufacturer, the redesigned process set up "order owners" as a single point of contact for all customers, from order generation to cash application. The result was much greater attention to accuracy and a direct relationship with the customer. Results were impressive. Cycle time for complete order processing went from seven days to twenty-four hours. Order change hand-offs (the number of times an order was passed to another individual to record and respond to customer changes) were cut from an average of fourteen to an average of two. Reduced inventory deductions and increased promotional activity were also features of the reengineered process. The people involved agreed that the new system was less stressful and more rewarding as they observed all metrics improving. Customers responded with substantially higher service ratings.

Another example involved a major food processor that decided to take a Level I look at operations planning and scheduling. For this firm, the objective was to develop an improved methodology that would provide a competitive advantage. The team formed for this assignment established five issues to be analyzed and addressed:

▶ Lack of planning tools to guide the manufacturing and delivery process effectively
▶ Reliance on rules of thumb for decision making
▶ Insufficient measures of performance
▶ Excessive dependence on individual evaluation and judgment
▶ No systematic forecasting of promotional lift (additional sales resulting from special promotions)

A flowchart of the existing process was created as a guide for redesign. The process began with a demand forecast, flowing then (through a material resource planning system) to inventory planning, production planning, master production scheduling, and finally detailed scheduling. Safety stocks were introduced between inventory planning and master production scheduling, and prebuilds were entered through sourcing for planned promotional activity. The flow also encompassed the planning and scheduling function. To reengineer the process for higher-level efficiency, the team applied "what if?" analysis to develop alternative solutions.

Beginning with the detailed analysis of existing processes, the team enthusiastically suggested novel changes and elimination of non-value-adding steps. Innovative thinking was encouraged throughout the effort. Time and again, the flowchart was dissected to identify steps that contributed nothing to satisfying customer needs. Simplification took precedence over sophistication. Cycle time reduction became a guiding factor, as did the potential to shave inventory not necessary to keep fill rates and delivery times at acceptable standards. Several revised flowcharts, each with significantly fewer process steps, were analyzed intensely (often with the help of interested outside parties) and discarded or amended in favor of more streamlined and effective systems. The process steps were eventually reduced by more than 50 percent.

> *Time and again, the flowchart was dissected to identify steps that contributed nothing to satisfying customer needs.*

The results of this Level I activity were a substantially more efficient operations planning approach, a onetime inventory reduction of $43 million, and an annual cost savings estimated at $15 million through the elimination of warehousing space.

▶ Other Level I Categories

The *tools* applied in the first level of supply chain management generally center on teaming techniques. Most organizations cannot overcome the strong temptation to begin internally and focus on favorite departments or processes. Functions such as purchasing, logistics, and freight are obvious choices. The teams use storyboarding (the building of a rough picture of the current work activities or process steps), process flow diagrams, scientific methods of decision making, and other tools to energize a group. Encouragement and support from senior management are crucial in these early stages because creative innovations may lead to significant improvements in stale processes.

The *action area* occurs in the midsection of the organization as functional managers and directors bear the brunt of the responsibility for implementing the new processes. Purchasing managers know the intensity with which cost containment is pursued in these initial efforts. As other departments come under the redesign microscope, the number of involved managers increases. Team members tend to come from a narrow band within the white-collar sector of the organization, only to be augmented later by blue-collar workers with more intimate knowledge of how work flows actually happen.

Guidance comes from whatever cost or financial data can be accessed. Often a company relies on the available internal metrics used to measure the performance of a function or department. Early results show that information is often in "ballpark ranges" at first but becomes more accurate as the savings are quantified, challenged, and recalculated to provide accurate results and promote funding for further efforts. Teams learn fairly rapidly, however, and begin to seek and find more useful financial data to support their hypotheses. Some rudiments of activity-based costing may be applied at this stage, but that approach is generally not part of the analysis until later levels.

Interest now focuses on manufacturing and delivery systems. Areas that would not normally come under the attention of purchasing but still involve significant cost are investigated. A major steel manufacturer illustrates the benefits to be found. This company developed an objective to redesign the maintenance, repair, and operating supplies (MRO) inventory and purchasing processes. The team formed was cross-functional with some guidance from outside consultants. The issues isolated by the focus team included these:

▶ Too much local inventory with slow usage and low turnover
▶ Duplicate parts in separate storage areas
▶ "Gut feel" replenishment targets, sourced through a manual system
▶ Large number of obsolete items still being inventoried and occasionally replenished

The first steps were to gather information on exactly what was in the current MRO inventory, who was ordering replacement goods, who the suppliers were, what quantities were ordered, and what prices were being charged. The first surprise came in the number of people doing the buying, many of whom were not authorized to make purchases. The second surprise was the number of suppliers for each item, in some cases as many as ten for a single item. In both instances, substantial reductions were an early result. With the information on the range of pricing, team members worked with the low-cost suppliers to determine that quality was not an issue. They then worked with the favored suppliers to bring supply down to one source for major categories. Next the team determined that one or two suppliers were able to take actual control for the MRO function. That meant giving these suppliers ownership of the stockroom in which the supplies were held and full responsibility for replenishment. In essence, the team determined it would be more beneficial for the steel firm to outsource the MRO function than to keep it internally. One-half the space normally allotted to storage and delivery of MRO supplies was leased to the selected suppliers. These external firms then took ownership of the inventory, in many instances eliminating half or more of the stock; established a disbursement system satisfactory to the mill personnel; and replenished directly from their distribution centers based on actual consumption.

Some complementary benefits included formalized inventory management practices with specific numbering for parts and services, perpetual inventory with high accuracy and a global inventory view, and standardized parts identification, bar coding, and digitized drawings. The key measured results were a projected reduction in spare parts inventory of 20 percent and reduced costs of 8 percent across an annual cycle of purchases.

▶ Modeling, Alliances, and Training

No formal *model* is customarily used in the first level. The teams typically create their own methodology, following generally prescribed teaming techniques. A simple flowchart or block diagram might be used to stimulate the brainstorming of ideas. Such diagrams show the transfer of products and services along the supply chain and focus

No formal model is customarily used in the first level.

discussions on problems and opportunities. Brainstorming sessions are used to analyze these rudimentary drawings and to assess opportunities for improvement. On the basis of these sessions, a list of prioritized opportunities is drawn up so that the best potential initiatives can be selected and implementation teams formed.

With an increased level of cross-functional cooperation, the teams find that outside help and fresh advice can be very beneficial. Some supplier consolidations occur as the supply base is reduced, and the seeds of longer-term *alliances* are planted with some of the surviving suppliers. Idea generation programs are initiated with key suppliers to find savings. A few of the more ambitious teams begin inviting representatives from the supply base to offer suggestions at team meetings, but real cross-company participation is held off until Level II.

The *training* effort is focused mostly on developing capabilities in team formation, problem identification, root-cause analysis, and the other elements of good teaming work in the early stages. Teams are sent out in a perpetual search for improvement opportunities. A few are even rewarded for finding such savings. The teams enlarge their scope as success is achieved and begin to rely on outside advice as they search for higher levels of savings.

The Full Supply Chain

When the organization gains skills through practice with supply chain initiatives, it extends the scope of its efforts beyond the traditional areas mentioned. Purchasing and logistics get a breather when teams extend their reach into more downstream areas and into the supply chain as a total system. A global leader in the supply of chemicals to industry offers an example of how these latter features are combined into a larger-scale Level I effort. This supplier was positioned at the front end of the supply chain because it provided supplies for downstream manufacturers and converters.

Exhibit 2.2 is a simplified flowchart of this firm's supply chain. Chemicals are produced at specialized plants and transported to manufacturing sites for processing and packaging. Some contract (toll) manufacturing is involved, in which another firm's chemicals are processed. Since the scope is international, product is shipped by sea to various ports of entry for transfer of chemicals to the manufacturing sites. From these sites, the final products are transported to industrial customers.

This supplier performed a distribution network analysis to determine the least-cost and best-service option. Such studies become more the norm as a firm develops supply chain skills and begins looking at the total organization. A secondary objective was to perform an inventory rationalization study, determining the correct A-B-C stratification (high-medium-lower priority) at the stock-keeping unit (SKU) level, and to set inventory improvement targets. The team drew a process flow map, in much greater detail than in Exhibit 2.2, and filled in the actual flows of material and the inventory levels maintained at each plant and manufacturing site. Service levels were analyzed by major customers, revealing a wide range in delivery performance.

The project parameters determined by the team included 107 package warehouses; thirty manufacturing sites; up to six warehouses

EXHIBIT 2.2

Case Study: Global Leader in the Supply of Chemicals to Industry

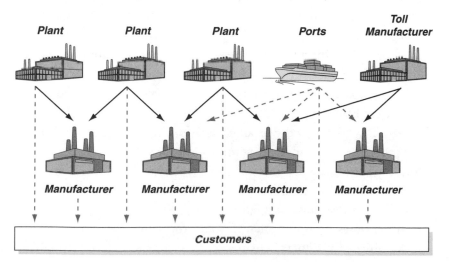

per city, with partial occupancy in many locations; fifteen independent business units within the firm; 150 customer consignment warehouses; average finished-goods inventory of $200 million; and over four thousand finished-goods SKUs.

Following a thorough analysis and redesign in which the team applied linear programming techniques to optimize the routing and use of storage, the firm consolidated package warehouses by 45 percent, generating $12 million in annual savings. The software essentially simulated the flow patterns and considered a large number of options to make the necessary deliveries with high service levels but with considerably less storage space and the most direct routing. The team also developed an A-B-C stratified SKU-Level Inventory program in which priority criteria were applied to the most essential (and often most profitable) products. By flowing the most important products first, the firm reduced delivery time on A items to two days. Substantial improvements were also made to the B and C items, but much less intensity was found necessary for the C items. The firm implemented a risk assessment tool, determining the most effective route for chemical shipments, and identified $10 million in annual inventory savings and potential savings of $40 million. Finally, the team developed inventory–customer service trade-off curves for predicting inventory and service risk, reducing further the amount of safety stock without compromising service levels.

Another example of this phase of supply chain improvement occurred for a building supplies manufacturer. This organization looked at the middle of a total supply chain with a primarily internal focus. The objective was to restructure the distribution network and stocking policies to leverage economies of scale. Cost reductions were targeted, and dramatic improvements to customer service measures were planned.

Exhibit 2.3 shows the product flow for this manufacturer. Product moved from their primary mill operations (lumber sawing and forming) and from suppliers of parts (such as hinges, fittings, and other hardware) to several processing sites. Some of these sites were combined distribution and fabrication centers, and some were public warehouses. In the former, further processing was performed to make finished products. The goods were then transferred to retail customers and builders. These firms then sold their products to consumers, the ultimate end users. The supply network included 139 distribution centers with a wide variety of commodity and specialty products. One problem was an excessive use of partial truckloads and an inconsistent order cycle time.

This project began with the formation of a team that sought solutions that might have already been developed. A list of firms that had made similar studies and improvements was developed with the help of a consultant and suppliers of similar materials. Plant visits were made to extract information from these improved firms and to see firsthand what had been accomplished. Discussions with the personnel at the visited sites proved to be extremely valuable in anticipating problems with the necessary change process. Benchmarking data were gathered on comparable levels of performance in the industry to pinpoint the gaps between current practices and industry best practices. With this information as a guide, the team then began the arduous task of redesigning its flowchart to reflect the better practices and the ideas generated during the visits.

EXHIBIT 2.3
Case Study: Building Supplies Manufacturer

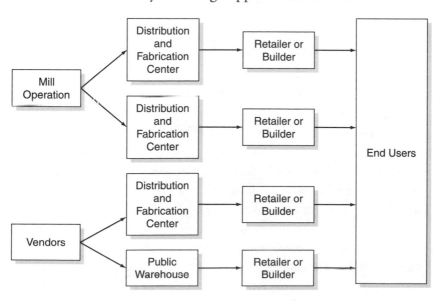

The team recommendations included the following:

▶ Stocking consolidation, allowed for by expanding from single-shift operation to multishift distribution center operations
▶ Reducing facilities from 139 to 50, keeping the most effective centers and shutting down those with high costs and poor delivery efficiency
▶ Specifying top-tier centers in the network as piece-pick and fabrication operations
▶ Assigning a second tier of network as stocking and sourcing facilities for high-volume and commodity products, cross-docking for piece-pick and fabrication products from top-tier facilities

The results were dramatic:

▶ 20 to 30 percent increased return on capital employed
▶ 30 to 50 percent sales, general, and administrative (SG&A) cost reduction through more efficient customer response and far less expediting
▶ Next-day delivery of full-truckload shipments and dedicated delivery days for less-than-truckload (LTL) shipments
▶ Leveraged product breadth and volume economies of scale

▶ Validation of Results

The improvements from Level I efforts are typically exaggerated but are genuine enough for most firms to continue the effort. Organizations completing a successful initial effort can typically cite a 10 to 15 percent improvement in purchasing costs. Inventories are reduced by 10 to 20 percent, and logistics costs are reduced 5 to 10 percent. There is some focus on cycle times, and white-collar costs might actually rise as employees and outside personnel are added to put new systems into place. More important, learning is extended, the process is validated, and soft areas of improvement are found that could have benefit for the organization equal to those documented under tangible cost savings.

▶ Conclusion: Work Remains After First-Level Efforts

For some industries and individual firms, the challenge to use supply chain development as an improvement technique still beckons. Utilities, telecommunication firms, hospitals, and banks are moving into areas already traversed by consumer products and manufacturing organizations. These industries have the opportunity to learn from the mistakes of the past or to repeat them as they progress to the higher levels of performance. The results show enormous opportunities, but pitfalls do exist.

For some industries and individual firms, the challenge to use supply chain development as an improvement technique still beckons.

As we consider the next levels in the evolution outlined in Exhibit 2.1, it is useful to consider firms that made successful ventures in Level I and point out some of the work left undone (the subject of the next chapter). For now, the lesson is that a supply chain improvement initiative offers a great opportunity to cross over all of the functions within an organization in order to build a network of supply that will differentiate the firm in the eyes of the customer. Level I is the stage in which that network begins to emerge. However, a significant amount of work must be performed to prevent the effort from deteriorating into an internal-only fix and to move logically to the next stages of improvement.

 *Chapter 3*

The Difficult Transition to Level II

Once a business organization has discovered the early, primarily internal benefits available from improvements within a supply chain, it can move to the next phase. Unfortunately, however, this transition to a higher level of supply chain management is difficult for some organizations.

The tendency is to get stuck in the early and relatively easy stages of the process, spasmodically pursuing departmentally oriented projects that require minimal cross-functional or interenterprise cooperation. Most firms continue to find other projects that will enhance internal supply chain performance but never really move on to higher-order efforts and benefits. Before considering the second level in the evolution being suggested, consideration should be given to the pitfalls and reasons behind this lack of progress.

▶ Conquering the Obstacles

Although the studies mentioned in Chapter 2 indicated significant improvement for the organizations, these cases represent onetime project redesign results. The recommended changes are beneficial, implementation leads to documented savings, and the savings can be used to fund future efforts, but the impetus to move to advanced levels is not assured. A firm might decide to improve order fulfillment, for example, but not capitalize by using these improved features to build new sales. Another organization might make dramatic changes to its warehousing and distribution system but fail to use these advantages to secure long-term gains in new markets.

Engineering, manufacturing, sales, and finance might work together on an early initiative and then fail to cooperate on solving long-standing problems. Still other firms will significantly reduce costs and eliminate non-value-adding steps in a delivery process and not take advantage of the additional capacity the redesigned system offers. In short, the firms remaining at Level I have a narrow vision of the full scope of supply chain management. This limited vision stays focused on how to make onetime process improvements to the internal infrastructure, systems, and methodologies, focusing primarily on cost reduction. Linking supply and demand across an entire network remains elusive for these companies.

> *In short, the firms remaining at Level I have a narrow vision of the full scope of supply chain management.*

To make further progress requires redesigning the total supply chain system and eventually the total supply chain network (in Levels III and IV). Standing in the way of progress are several pitfalls that keep a firm mired in Level I. The organization interested in reaching advanced levels must identify these obstacles and overcome them. Let us examine some of the most formidable pitfalls.

▶ *A natural resistance to change exists in some organizations, often exacerbated by a "not invented here" culture.* Internal inertia dictates the pace of change in every company. Every firm in the sample studied for this book had a continuous improvement effort in progress. Some move ahead faster; others go more slowly. To drive an organization to higher levels of cost reduction, productivity, quality, and service, energy must come typically from one or more of three sources:

executive motivation, a system that tracks progress and rewards the people who made it happen, and a vision that embraces ongoing change in the future. Though most firms today have one or more of these three in place, companies vary greatly in intensity, consistency, and results achieved.

▶ *Most firms stuck in Level I typified this variation, foremost by refusing to share savings from the improvement effort.* For these companies, the guiding principle goes something like this: "The change initiatives had to be done to secure jobs." As senior managers fed lavishly at the end-of-year trough by giving themselves large bonuses for the improvements achieved, most of the people who had invested the extra effort necessary to make the improvements lost motivation, and the efforts stalled. Sharing the real savings is a mark of the organizations that progress to Level II and beyond.

▶ *Insufficient resources delay progress.* With so much downsizing in organizations over the past decade or more, few companies have the resources needed to pursue all improvement opportunities. Securing enough qualified people to form high-potential action teams has become a limiting factor. Typically, a Level I firm will not allocate, hire, or contract with the people necessary to move to the next level. It is far easier for these firms simply to ignore the advanced opportunities, under the guise that they are not worth the extra expenditures, or to stall efforts until internal resources can be developed and applied. This practice unfortunately tends to block such firms at the lowest stage of evolution.

Firms that advance beyond Level I discover the necessary resources, often from suppliers, distributors, and customers interested in making supply chain advances that help them create competitive advantage through a cooperative network. Others simply make the investments needed to build such a network and ensure future advantage, regardless of the cost. This latter effort requires courage and risk-taking ability often lacking in the organizations stuck at Level I.

▶ *Withdrawal of executive involvement signals satisfaction with the status quo.* There is always enthusiasm in the beginning of supply chain improvement efforts. As that enthusiasm ebbs and senior sponsors return to their normal areas of activity, the people involved in planning further progress take time to breathe a little easier. This stalls progress. Studies show that it is not for want of results that executives withdraw their direct support. It is more often simply a case of losing interest in a process that these executives assume to be self-perpetuating. That assumption is usually fatal to progress.

▶ *Only when there is visible and continued emphasis on process improvement at the highest levels will there be continued progress.* The natural tendency in a business organization is to seek a level of equilibrium in which the players pursue their normal roles without pressure for quantum leaps forward. Level I firms quickly reach that equilibrium when senior management rests on early results. Movement to Level II requires a renewed intensity oriented around corporate objectives that make sense to the improvement teams. This simple lesson eludes most Level I firms.

▶ *Overlooking poor forecasts inhibits the degree of improvement that can be achieved.* A specific characteristic of Level I efforts is progress in virtually all areas of supply chain management, except one—forecast accuracy. Getting better information into a supply system regarding how much actual demand will exist in a specific time frame is a universal challenge. Manufacturing and delivery efficiency are directly correlated with the accuracy of this information, but firms continue to accept accuracy below 50 percent. Sales representatives responsible for polling customers to determine estimated purchases will accept virtually any number and neglect to enter information on expected changes at a major customer. Buyers asked for sales predictions will provide last year's numbers. Sales managers will increase the numbers if the aggregate does not match budget. Vice presidents will increase the numbers further just because they are vice presidents. Left uncontrolled, it becomes a fool's game in which schedules and plans are made and never kept. Level I organizations will brush the issue aside. In the process, they doom themselves to staying in the lower levels of progress. With poor demand input, the planning process relies on educated guessing at best. The resulting system works only because of heroic service, not organized reaction. Level I firms are always responding to unexpected changes. Job security seems to reside in the special service actions taken to satisfy the whims of customers. Progress to Level II is inhibited by the perception that the situation simply cannot be improved. As we consider

Level II progress, however, we will find that a great deal can be done to improve forecast accuracy.

▶ *The tendency to apply technology reactively results in poor information technology (IT) alignment.* An argument always raised in Level I efforts revolves around what should happen first, the installation of new information systems or the redesign of processes for higher efficiency. The greatest gains occur when the redesign of the process is logically tested and aligned properly with the IT application. For Level I firms, the tendency is to develop process improvements and technology enhancements in vacuums, without any real integration. Advancing to the next level requires the functional groups and the IT department to codesign the new processes with what will be the best IT format.

A typical situation encountered at Level I is a firm struggling with a hodgepodge of software that does not interface with what operations needs and requires significant manual override to move information among and between systems and processes. In discussing the later stages of supply chain evolution, we will examine the importance of technology and its sequential application in detail. For now, the point to stress is that higher levels of progress involve technology solutions that proactively support the new process designs.

▶ *Lack of trust causes potential supply chain allies to withhold expertise and inhibit cooperation.* The single greatest obstacle to advanced supply chain improvement is a lack of trust among the parties who will most benefit from cooperation in pursuing mutual goals. Supply chain improvement by its very nature requires total cooperation. Departments have to work together. Key suppliers have to play a role in design and application. Distributors have to play another role in handling small lots and specialized market sectors. Customers have to help determine what should be coming through the chain. And every constituent has to listen to the voice of the ultimate consumer and make certain that the network is responding properly.

Firms stuck at this level remain unwilling to exercise the cooperation, interaction, and progressive vision that are essential to achieving the major savings and competitive advantage available at higher levels.

Such a situation cries out for interaction, but this seldom happens in Level I. Savings do occur, but every constituent so covets the benefits for his or her own organization that trust remains elusive. Buyers want to dominate the negotiations. Sellers resist giving more improvement ideas. In short, the concept of win-lose dominates Level I. Firms stuck at this level remain unwilling to exercise the cooperation, interaction, and progressive vision that are essential to achieving the major savings and competitive advantage available at higher levels.

In one experience with a large retailer, solidly mired in Level I, the request was to help the firm find additional areas of improvement. There were already documented savings, hypothetically as a result of strong purchase leveraging with a smaller supply base. The executives wanted to move forward, using the experience as a guide to "higher-order" savings. The suggestion was to form a pilot study, in which a small group of suppliers and distributors would work with the retailer to develop a prioritized list of improvements that could benefit all parties. When another suggestion was made that these savings should be shared with all parties, to create an incentive for producing ideas, the retailer balked, contending that the purpose was to improve its own profits, not those of suppliers and distributors.

The effort was hopeless. The retailer's reputation interfered at every step. When calls were made to potential suppliers, even those with which a long-term relationship existed, the response was the same: they simply refused to work on any pilot program with this particular retailer. Further investigation led to an interesting revelation. Despite claims of superior negotiating skills, the retailer was not receiving the lowest prices on purchased products. Because the suppliers expected to be badgered for big discounts by the retailer's purchasing group, the suppliers simply raised the initial offering price. The retailer was comfortable in the perception that it had the lowest prices in the market, but its buyers were fooling no one but themselves. When evidence was presented concerning these facts, the company simply denied the validity of the data. The pilot never occurred, and the firm continues to look for suppliers to badger. If such behavior continues, this firm will remain at Level I perpetually.

▶ Attitude and Progress

One result of post–Level I efforts is that the supply chain rises in importance, from a collection of cost centers working independently and needing constant improvement to a strategic resource that can enable competitive advantage. Executive endorsement and cross-functional effort are the catalysts in this change, but progress to a higher level will be limited unless an organization develops a mind-set that challenges the firm to capitalize on the momentum. This thinking must be oriented around how a firm can take the collective resources of the supply network, with the enthusiasm generated by early results, and build not just an effective internal system but a competitively advantaged supply network linked with external partners. Developing such a mind-set is not easy and often eludes first-level companies.

In the early stages of development, there is good news and bad news. The good news is that the firm practicing supply chain improvement for the first time discovers the value of looking holistically at its business, from initial supply to final consumption, and realizes that there are benefits to be gained across the entire system. The emerging scenario reveals an enterprise that can be continuously improved and that pleases its customers. The tools and techniques for enabling advanced improvement (process mapping, teaming, process redesign, and so on) are developed and proven. The teams usually have fun working together, developing the changes that make better systems, and recording the better results in areas of purchasing, transportation, inventory, and warehousing. A new sense of camaraderie appears in most organizations. A concept of total organizational change for the better emerges. It is a time to capitalize on the effort and create a long-term business plan built around the successes. It provides a chance to restore the concept of loyalty as the firm and all its supply chain participants can benefit because the future is secured through a superior customer satisfaction network.

The bad news, for organizations that stall, is that this learning is not translated into a guiding format, an organizational mind-set.

Much work always remains after the early gains. Some firms will succeed; others will not. The former group turns the supply chain into a driving force that can guide improvement for years by constantly updating the improvement list and seeking out better practices in other organizations. The successes achieved draw the constituents together and take them to advanced efforts. The latter group accepts the results as a onetime success and goes back to business as usual. These firms fail to grasp that a supply chain strategy can provide a significant competitive advantage. They prefer to think any advantage comes from the skills of the leaders and the expertise of the organizational departments. An appalling arrogance permeates most of these firms, exuding a baseless confidence in their systems and infrastructure as though thoughts of improvement were no longer necessary.

Organizations dictating that all savings from the improvement efforts be divided only among the most senior executives and those holding shares in the company doom their firms to stay in the first level of evolution. Rewards must be set aside for the suppliers, employees, distributors, and others who help achieve the advanced levels of progress. There will be plenty left over for the shareholders as the higher stages focus on increasing shareholder value. Crossing the first bridge, however, requires that leaders in the firm show the way to the future and reward the players for acting out their roles in the journey.

> *Crossing the first bridge, however, requires that leaders in the firm show the way to the future and reward the players for acting out their roles in the journey.*

Unfortunately, some companies simply miss the point at this early crossing. When a reputable survey was conducted of over two hundred organizations engaged in manufacturing, distribution, and retailing, 89 percent of the respondents said they viewed the supply chain as a holistic system and as a means of gaining competitive advantage. When asked if the organization had a supply chain executive, 52 percent replied in the negative; 92 percent of the sample reported that the supply chain would influence their business strategy, but few could cite any specific strategic initiatives based on the concept.

▶ Clear Vision

Developing a vision that guides a supply chain improvement effort toward an optimized network position requires joining together all interacting constituents and mutually developing the proper focus. Dictating the vision from the top will yield short-term progress, but long-term success depends on both top-down and bottom-up interaction. The goal should be to pursue—and share—the full benefits of supply chain excellence. That movement proceeds as follows.

▶ *Consider the next wave of optimization. Think together how an advantaged chain is going to look five to ten years from now.* Focus groups made up of constituents across the supply chain can come together and think out to the future, speculating about what conditions will prevail among the market leaders. One successful technique is to arrange what I call a "partnering diagnostic laboratory." In such labs, representatives from design, engineering, manufacturing, planning, sales, marketing, and finance—with a key supplier, an important distributor, and a focused customer—meet for about two days to discuss together how the firm can improve its supply chain efforts. Experience has shown that valuable insights that would not normally be exchanged under typical relationships spill out at such focus sessions, especially under the guidance of a skilled facilitator.

Call the group "vision seekers" and commission them to come back with a model of what the next wave of improvement efforts will bring. Let them get as wild as they want. Encourage innovation. Make certain that they consider technology as a tool of implementation.

▶ *Define what "supply chain" means.* As the suggestions come back, create a clear definition of what *supply chain* means for your particular organization. That is the start of a driving vision. For some firms, the supply chain includes all major supplies (from the 20 percent of key suppliers of 80 percent of the things that make up most of the cost of goods sold), through manufacture and distribution, to a select group of targeted customers. This definition will suffice for a start. It can be expanded as the firm advances in implementation. Higher-level firms invariably add to the definition technological features that speed up data exchange and enhance the response capability of the supply chain. A simple picture or illustration always helps participants focus on just what the organization is trying to improve. Eventually a supply chain model appears that captures the essence of the effort for the firm's people.

One manufacturing organization that made a rapid advance from Level I to Level II took the time to gather its various internal functions and asked a professional adviser to join them and seriously critique its progress in view of what other organizations, inside and outside the industry, had accomplished. They reviewed past efforts and evaluated planned initiatives. In an open forum, emphasizing honesty about both positive and negative views, the group members determined where accomplishments had been made and where they had failed with their supply chain effort. Most important, they determined where they thought the effort could be extended.

After some gut-wrenching revelations, the manufacturer concluded that fewer than half of the potential improvements had been achieved and that further gains would be limited by the lack of a vision that would unite internal functions in a joint effort. Each function had made some progress, mainly in purchasing, inventory, and transportation, but an equal additional gain was still possible. The solution became how to define the total supply chain as a future survival tactic, but this solution depended on help from key allies. This total effort required a focus clearly spelled out in sharing sessions. At these sessions, representatives of all the involved functions came together as peers to define consumption patterns in the industry, determine where the trends were headed, and discuss the benefits of a cooperative effort. Although the participants did not achieve an external effort (that had to wait until Level III), they did find significant areas in which further work, with the help of external resources, would enhance company performance.

▶ *Expand the meaning by mapping the full supply chain process.* As a follow-up to the sharing sessions, the group mentioned above took considerable time and effort to map the supply process together so that the potential partners could see where mutual efforts might build a stronger network. The number of key suppliers and distributors necessary to gain an advantage became smaller than expected, and Level II types of initiatives were born. At this point, it might appear as though the effort were moving to Levels III and IV (the external part of the evolution), but it is not. The effort was still focused on improving internal systems, particularly for the manufacturer. But enough learning was taking place to plant the seeds for future external cooperation. In the interim, the manufacturer was able to link up with key organizations to advance the improvements made in its early efforts and to begin working seriously with interested allies across the entire supply chain.

▶ *Drive innovation. Use outside counsel.* The real secret is to encourage fresh thinking. In Level I there will be progress, but it tends to be restricted to the areas mentioned. Reaching a higher level requires ingenuity. Since most organizations suffer from a myopic view of how improvements should be pursued, outside advice must be obtained. Specialists, industry experts, or consultants can help in this effort. Encourage the participants to go as deep as they want, gather as much information as necessary, visit firms in other industries that have made good progress, and at all times keep their thinking freewheeling and fresh.

> **The real secret is to encourage fresh thinking.**

▶ *Ensure the technology connection with a supporting strategy and plan.* As the supply chain of the future emerges, a company must reach out for appropriate technology that will enhance its advantage. Later in this book, advanced concepts will be defined at length. At this stage, some expert guidance is advisable to make certain that the necessary information technology is being developed as the key processes are being redesigned. This advice can come from experienced practitioners, consultants, and industry experts. In many industries, conferences are held at which informed speakers give insights into what is working and what is not. Attending such conferences or simply reading the appropriate literature is essential.

▶ *Organize a pilot program to crystallize the vision.* Since few firms will move into advanced levels without a clear sign of payback, a pilot study to prove the value of the new ideas is always a good idea. This pilot should be in an area where the findings will be representative and the results will show whether the concepts are viable or not. Pilots are described in greater detail in Chapter 4; essentially, they consist of selecting a particular business unit, specific factory, or product line and creating a 90- to 120-day experiment in which various supply chain improvement techniques are tested and monitored to determine actual savings. These pilots go a long way toward quieting the naysaying critics who may try to stymie early improvement efforts.

▶ *Spell out the vision in easily understandable terms.* A compelling vision will include the interenterprise network that will be improved and should contain such goals as "creating a customer satisfaction-driven supply chain network in which alliances are established to optimize the inherent processes," "providing maximum value to the ultimate consumer while allowing network partners to enhance profitability," and "establishing a proactive, evolving, continually improving model that can be applied in many markets."

To make this vision a reality, the company must change traditional roles, particularly between the buyers and sellers in the early stages of progress, internally and externally. The buyers must become analysts, strategists, and negotiators rather than gatekeepers and guardians. Suppliers must assume a critical responsibility for satisfying the demands of all customers. They must become proactive, cooperative, and innovative rather than merely reactive.

▶ Setting the Stage for the Next Transition

With a clear vision for continuing the supply chain effort and a determination to reach the higher levels, a firm is ready for the next stage of the evolution. The process will continue in an internal mode, but the tools and techniques will be enhanced and prepare the organization for the external mode. The characteristics of this second level will be described in Chapter 4. To sum up this chapter, the key point is that it takes dedication to use supply chain improvement as a mechanism that crosses all organizational functions and requires total internal cooperation to achieve full benefits.

 *Chapter 4*

Moving to the Second Level of Progress

Once a firm has realized that supply chain improvement is an important vehicle to make further gains across all activities of an organization and is determined to bring a higher dimension to the concept of cross-functional cooperation, it is ready to move to the second level of the progress. In this level, the firm will sustain a primarily *internal* focus but will find additional areas of concentration and new ways in which specialized teams can develop savings that would otherwise be overlooked in normal process improvement efforts. Suppliers will begin to play a larger and more important role in the activities, but generally under the control of the purchasing function, and with all savings accruing to the buyer. (In later levels of progress, the supplier activity becomes much freer and more open as savings are shared.) Technology will begin to play a greater role in the initiatives, and results will be monitored and measured much more precisely.

The supply chain is really a mechanism for fulfilling demand, and a key enabler of that process in Level II becomes the uninhibited flow of accurate information across the supply network. Organizations that move beyond the limited early efforts begin to understand that the demand fulfillment network, of which they are a part, cannot be optimized without state-of-the-art information technology that correctly links supply with demand. Optimization requires reliable electronic data interchange across the entire system; a single bottleneck impeding information transfer disadvantages the entire network. Building a totally integrated information pipeline begins in Level II. The organization recognizes the severe limitations of its information system and begins to design something useful for internal purposes before trying to integrate with more advanced external parties.

> *Organizations that move beyond the limited early efforts begin to understand that the demand fulfillment network, of which they are a part, cannot be optimized without state-of-the-art information technology that correctly links supply with demand.*

The organization begins to make important investments in supply chain information technology. Much of this investment will be directed toward integration of internal business systems. In a survey of two hundred firms at Level II, 45 percent indicated they were taking an enterprise resource planning (ERP) approach to their future supply chain systems, developing an integrated package of business solutions and customizing their approach to the market. These systems are at the center of efforts to integrate various internal functions and eliminate much of the inefficiency that exists in Level I and II firms. Speed of implementation of ERP becomes important as Level III and IV firms advance beyond the mere integration of software for internal purposes and move toward creating global networks for planning and delivery. In the future, planning will be integrated so that the various constituencies in a supply chain will be drawn together in a total effort, generally focused on specific markets and key customers.

The wider scope, the greater demand for resources to implement the required actions, and the time needed to implement these integrated systems will delay some firms from making the necessary commitment to build a more *customer-focused* system and infrastructure.

These firms will not complete the work in Level II or make the transition to Level III. With an enlarged understanding and a commitment to find and allocate the necessary resources, in an environment built on enabling technology, some firms will prepare for the next step in the evolution and progress through Level II.

▶ An Improvement Scenario

A driving force behind Level II efforts comes from the realization that gains beyond those derived from normal cost reduction are feasible. The firms that have made the transition to the second stage of evolution understand that from a large variety of supply chain alternatives, a plan for successful implementation can emerge. This plan brings profitable revenue growth as well as cost containment and should have the following distinct features.

▶ *Cycle times can drop dramatically—in many cases to hours.* For most firms, a reduction in the time to complete a cycle—from order to delivery, from new idea to commercialization, from order entry to receipt of cash, and so forth—can mean a significant gain in new business that brings more income and cash flow. Level II supply chain efforts generally lead to improvements in these cycles on the order of 40 to 50 percent. A cycle to fill an order of thirty days could be cut to fifteen, lead times of two to three weeks can be slashed to one week (in best-case situations to days), the time to introduce a new product can be cut from twenty-four months to twelve.

One firm that leased computer hardware reduced the time to fulfill an order from thirty days to eight hours by eliminating all of the approval delays and automating the order management process. With this improvement, the sales force was able to gain new orders that were being lost to faster-responding competitors. Processing of claims for an insurance firm that used to take days was reduced to hours by empowering the employees to make decisions within their capability, training them to take a more proactive posture when dealing with customers, and arming them first with significant data via an intranet (within-firm) communication system that gave quick access to best past practices.

▶ *Errors can be minimized; inspection can be reduced.* One of the biggest findings in Level II is that a large number of mistakes and errors are made within most systems. Some firms found at least one error in more than half of all incoming orders. Old legacy systems (computer software that has been on-line for some time and functioning as a standalone entity) in the information processing area have been found to be a source of mistakes at the hand-off points between systems. Pricing is a common source of errors, but most can be eliminated. A focus on why they exist and the building of fail-safe systems can boost confidence and accuracy rates to well over 90 percent. With this improvement comes a better relationship with customers, who often go elsewhere with their orders when frustrated by errors in a system.

Inspection, to maintain quality, can also be reduced. Working with key supplier groups that have demonstrated quality levels, documented by such practices as certification by the ISO, the international quality standards organization, can dramatically reduce the inconsistencies of supply and the need to check all incoming materials.

▶ *Inventories can be slashed; safety stocks can be reduced.* A key finding from Level I efforts was that despite high inventory levels, orders were missed because the right product was not available at the right time. A second finding was that a serious amount of redundant material was in the safety stock intended to overcome this inefficiency. Level II firms develop the means to have lower amounts of the right inventory and, in the process, satisfy the customer better. With these improvements, stockouts can be reduced dramatically and sales increased.

One major consumer products firm analyzed how much revenue could be increased by always having the demanded stock available. The study evaluated how much business was lost during a specific test period because the right goods were not available (in spite of high levels of safety stocks). The conclusion was an improvement of 9 percent. Another firm took a larger, network view and discovered that an equal amount of safety stock was held by its distributors. Neither constituent (manufacturer or distributor) trusted the existing system to have enough stock when needed, so both carried excess inventories. The new system, based on improved forecast accuracy through implementation of software designed for that purpose, cut those inventories by more than half, resulting in substantial savings for both constituents while sustaining or increasing customer service levels.

▶ *Paperwork can be minimized.* When a firm takes a serious look at the amount of paperwork that supports its operations, it often discovers that most of the paper is an attempt to cover the inefficiency of the current systems. Firms in Level II find that much of the paperwork can be automated or eliminated. With this reduction in time-consuming documentation comes an opportunity to focus on getting new orders and serving customers.

The process begins in order entry, where most of the transactions can be automated. Purchasing is another opportunity area, since purchase orders, acknowledgments, and receiving information can be done electronically. Invoicing and payments are another area. More advanced firms simply go in search of the means to introduce paperless (and error-free) systems to their business at key transaction points (for example, purchases, messages, master scheduling, invoicing, and payments).

▶ *Best-selling items can always be available.* Reduction of inventories has been mentioned. A corollary effect is having the best-selling items always available. This is done by linking consumption (actual demand) with supply in such a way that the firm pulls the right product and service to the point of demand. Replenishment systems based on pull, backed with the necessary electronic data interchange and reliable information, will accomplish this task. Wal-Mart's replenishment is now automatically triggered when product is sold.

> Customers are drawn to this type of network because of the ease of doing business.

▶ *Value enhancement can be shared across the network.* As these features are introduced, the entire network of supply is improved. Customers are drawn to this type of network because of the ease of doing business. One hidden benefit has been the realization that there is virtually nothing in the supply chain that cannot be improved.

Enhancements start to multiply as efficiency becomes a fact instead of a fancy. Revenues can only increase in such an environment.

▶ Internal Alliances

In Level II of the supply chain evolution, the effort to build cross-functional cooperation as a strategy for success will continue, largely influenced and enhanced by better information sharing. The organizational strategy and business plan will remain intact, but supplying the strategic information necessary to support implementing that plan will become an important goal. A parallel tactical information path will start to develop as units within the organization begin to realize the competitive advantage of having correct, timely information. These information paths will create a free-flowing and visible data stream across the internal supply chain linking the various functions so that people know what is happening throughout the organization. Old adversaries in the organization become genuine allies.

Progressing in Level II requires establishing a free flow of reliable information that can be used by the internal constituents in the supply chain to make better decisions and serve customers more effectively. This data flow becomes the lifeblood for those who make the higher-order improvements. For those organizations, the new customer focus, backed with a reliable two-way flow of information, is what links supply and demand, making optimization of the system possible. Wal-Mart's electronic data interchange (EDI) system is intimately matched with those of its approved suppliers. Replenishment information flows quickly and accurately, with dramatically reduced inventories supporting that replenishment. Funds transfer is swift and electronic. That kind of linkage is impossible until the manufacturer improves the capability of internal information systems to match that of its leading customers.

Exhibit 4.1 reproduces Exhibit 2.1 from Chapter 2. Notice that in Level II, the *driver* behind the process effort shifts. The purchasing department is not absolved from finding further savings. Indeed, studies show there is always some form of pressure on this function to seek novel ways to reduce costs. But in the next level, the emphasis

EXHIBIT 4.1
Level II: Internal Excellence

	Internal		External	
	Sourcing and Logistics I	**Internal Excellence II**	**Network Construction III**	**Industry Leadership IV**
Driver	VP sourcing (under pressure)	CIO/supply chain leader	Business unit leaders	Management team
Benefits	Leveraged savings	Prioritized improvements across network	Best partner performance	Network advantage, profitable revenue
Focus	Inventory, logistics, freight, order fulfillment	Process redesign, system improvement	Forecasting, planning, customer services, interenterprise	Consumer, network
Tools	Teaming, functional excellence	Benchmarks, best practice, activity-based costing	Metrics, database mining, electronic commerce	Intranet, Internet, virtual information systems
Action Area	Midlevel organization	Expanded levels	Total organization	Full enterprise
Guidance	Cost data, success funding	Process mapping	Advanced cost models, differentiating processes	Demand-supply linkage
Model	None	Supply chain—intraenterprise	Interenterprise	Global market
Alliances	Supplier consolidation	Best partner	Formal alliances	Joint ventures
Training	Team	Leadership	Partnering	Network processing

shifts to working through the focused action teams to find greater internal gains and to build the systems necessary to bring an external perspective to the effort. These teams cannot be allowed to operate independently, however. The effort must be coordinated and integrated, or the results will be chaotic. In Level II, the role of driver typically shifts to a designated supply chain leader, usually with the help of the chief information officer (CIO), because supporting information technology is essential to success.

This leader's role is to pursue higher levels of internal excellence. Idea generation sessions with teams from across the firm produce valuable suggestions, particularly if a few external suppliers and industry experts are invited to give advice. Partnering diagnostic sessions are a tool for finding these suggestions. In such a focus group or analytical laboratory, experienced people assess the opportunities from improving current processes and systems. Case studies are reviewed for possible insights. Innovative models are created and critiqued. Ideas on new ways of doing business are always encouraged. A day or two is generally necessary to get an opportunity list started and refined. Then special focus teams can be assigned, using cross-functional resources, to pursue the highest-priority improvements.

▶ High-Payback Actions as a Focus

Once the company has established a supply chain leader and department, as well as internal alliances across functions, its next job is to evaluate alternative actions and priorities for actualizing the improvement opportunities. For example, software systems can build a virtual inventory that will contain accurate information on all inventory available to promise (ATP), no matter where it may exist. With that information, a sales representative or customer service representative dealing with a customer will be certain of the products scheduled for production, inventory in transit, inventory in stock, and inventory at distribution centers available for transfer. Such an ATP system can help a company dramatically increase revenues and reduce the costs of shipping and expediting. Other actions could include developing a shortened network of distribution that takes products more directly to the customer, bypassing warehousing, and the means to manage daily transportation on a worldwide scale.

Modern systems demand the electronic linkages and passing of information that gives the network an advantage over slower and less efficient networks.

As the search for improvements continues, information technology becomes increasingly crucial. Modern systems demand the electronic linkages and passing of information that gives the network an advantage over slower and less efficient networks. As the discernibly superior network forms, the firm begins to solidify its advantage in the market. The action teams focus on exploiting this advantage as the organization moves toward the external phase of the evolution.

As the business world continues to accelerate in the development of efficient electronic communications, processes within organizations must be streamlined to keep pace, or else the firm suffers a disadvantage. Quick access to reliable information, on an ever-increasing scale of operations, has become so important that a company simply cannot prosper, let alone lead, without superior data retrieval and reliability. The CIO role grows more important as the organization begins to understand this necessity and to study technologies that will enable process improvements beyond Level I. Processes must be streamlined, the redundancies eliminated, the errors and the non-value-adding features removed so that state-of-the-art technology can be more effectively applied. The seemingly infinite choice of available software and systems has to be evaluated to find the best fit for a particular firm.

Analyzing the "as is" condition of a process is generally the first step in the procedure. A team might analyze how the accounts payable department goes about paying the firm's bills. Start by interviewing employees and making flowcharts that depict how the process is done. Next, brainstorming and idea generation usually lead to a dramatic reduction of steps in the process. Human interventions are cut significantly, and cycle times are greatly reduced. Many improved systems applications usually accompany the changed process. One user described this experience with a redesign effort:

"'I've been in manufacturing for 20 years,' said Terry Gleason, a general manager at Thompson Consumer Electronics in Indianapolis, who has used supply chain software to cut its planning and scheduling staff from 22 people to four. 'This is the answer I've searched for my whole career'" (Stein, 1997, p. 45).

▶ Payback Opportunities Across the Network

The *benefits* in Level II begin to arrive from prioritized improvement efforts, based on a list of potential initiatives kept up-to-date by teams representing most of the organization. A few favorite departments will be left out in the beginning of the investigation, as some senior executives will strongly resist reengineering functions they have nurtured. Sales seems to be a particularly guarded area among Level II firms, even though improvements in this area can be very significant, particularly as the sales force is equipped with better data. As the optimization opportunities are pursued, even this area lands on the potential action list. The company needs to focus on the most attainable, most profitable opportunities, and this objective calls for evaluations of a much more penetrating nature. The teams are sent across all functions as the leaders begin looking at the full potential of the supply chain.

Exhibit 4.2 lists the opportunity areas of greatest interest in Level II. This list is not exhaustive but does include the initiatives with the highest potential for successful results. The list is also not in order of priority but rather sequential, arranged from the creation of a product or service through delivery and after-sale servicing. Each of the opportunity areas identified in the exhibit will be described in the text.

Beginning with *product development,* most firms have an adequate research and development group working with quality assurance and engineering to bring forth a flow of new products. From a supply chain perspective, the aim is to analyze closely the total time required from when an idea or concept is created until a commercialized product is being sold in the market. During this process, considerable emphasis is placed on developing a salable product or service by including the voice of the consumer in the design process. That

EXHIBIT 4.2
Supply Chain Optimization Opportunities

Product Development
- Concept-to-market
- Voice of the consumer

Forecasting
- Forecast accuracy
- Short-interval planning

Market Segmentation
- Profitable revenue growth

Sourcing
- Partnering
- Alliances
- Global aspects

Pricing

Order-to-Cash
- Order fulfillment
- Error elimination
- Inventory management

Enterprise Resource Planning

Logistics
- Warehousing
- Distribution
- Transportation

Electronic Commerce
- EDI
- IT fusion
- Sales for effectiveness

means that the team charged with reducing this particular cycle time does not make recommended improvements unless there is validation that the changes will result in a more favorably accepted alternative or new product.

A food products company studied the time for its bakery division to introduce a new pastry: twenty-four months from the beginning to the end of the commercialization cycle. That is not an unusual amount of time in the sample of companies studied. The action team charged with reducing this cycle worked diligently to eliminate steps that slowed the process. The first step was to get rid of the redundant approvals in the process and to force approval forward if delayed by a particular executive for more than five days. That change removed six months from the cycle. Next the team improved the computer-aided design (CAD) and computer-aided manufacturing (CAM) systems to make them more interactive and cut another three months. In a move that showed the advantage of external help, the team asked a few key suppliers for improvement ideas. One suggestion reduced cycle time by allowing suppliers to go forward with new designs concurrently with engineering changes. The end result was a cycle reduced to twelve months. A second effort in the company's Level III progression reduced cycles to less than six months for products identified as having a high probability of success.

Some keys to improvement included giving advance information to the suppliers of tooling and packaging to have the right supplies ready when the new product was out of prototype and into manufacturing. Another was the digitizing of the information that would go into the advertising, promotion, and packaging of the new products so that changes could be handled electronically. Samples of graphic design and packaging were also transferred via an electronic linkage, rather than by a physical means. At each step in the improvement, the consumers were consulted to make certain the product would meet their demands.

Forecasting is important to Level II improvement efforts. The manufacturing and delivery processes depend greatly on knowing how much demand exists. Forecast accuracy is often found to be as low as 30 to 40 percent. By working with customers, making much greater use of historical data, and linking current consumption information across the supply chain, Level II firms have found that forecast accuracy can be increased by 80 percent or more. One of the secrets is to move to a shorter planning horizon, in which current pull-through consumption information is used, rather than the speculative data usually applied. Under these conditions, the system is redesigned to work on shorter lead times across the network, with smaller inventories, so the company can respond much faster and more flexibly to what is happening at the point of consumption.

Special software programs can help immensely in this area. Firms such as i2 Technology and Manugistics have developed software that links information across the full chain of supply (Mentzer, 1997, is a very useful reference). With these improved systems, a manufacturer can relate incoming sales to the flow of supplies and conversion schedules to make realistic promises of delivery. Suppliers become so well linked that a particular order can be translated into a specific flow of materials. If a key supplier can fulfill only 90 percent of a particular need, that information flows immediately to the manufacturer, which then knows not to promise more than 90 percent of the completed order. Inventories can also be tracked over such systems, so critical reallocations can be made when necessary to fulfill a higher-priority order.

▶ A New Look at the Market and Customers

As a firm becomes more sophisticated in its supply chain knowledge and management, it must make certain that the improved processes are affecting the correct consumers in the correct way. To verify this, most firms make some sort of *market segmentation* effort a part of their Level II efforts. A special team is formed, often with senior executive participation, to analyze the various markets being served and to identify potential new ones to penetrate. Most firms are very arrogant in this respect, believing they know all there is to know about the particular markets they serve. Because they have participated in these markets for so long, they also resist information that shows market deterioration, major changes in buying patterns, or a lack of future growth possibilities.

> **Most firms are very arrogant in this respect, believing they know all there is to know about the particular markets they serve.**

Exhibit 4.3 shows an analogy used many times to focus the proper attention on this important area of supply chain opportunity. The contention is that most firms sell "dragons," whether they realize it or not. Using this analogy, the depiction starts with the head of the dragon, the fire-breathing fearsome part that strikes terror in the observer. The chart drawn shows the head contains the category A customers, representing (for this illustration) about 15 percent of the

EXHIBIT 4.3

The Customer Dragon

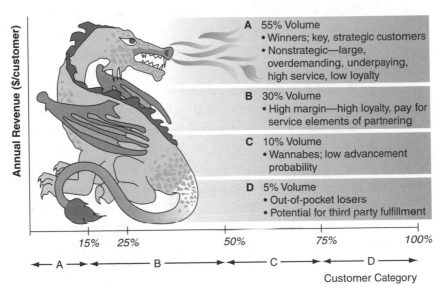

Annual Revenue ($/customer)

A 55% Volume
- Winners; key, strategic customers
- Nonstrategic—large, overdemanding, underpaying, high service, low loyalty

B 30% Volume
- High margin—high loyalty, pay for service elements of partnering

C 10% Volume
- Wannabes; low advancement probability

D 5% Volume
- Out-of-pocket losers
- Potential for third party fulfillment

15%   25%   50%   75%   100%

← A → ← B → ← C → ← D →

Customer Category

number of customers but about 55 percent of the total sales volume. This head contains many "winners," customers that are key to the firm's future strategy and long-term growth potential.

Repeated analyses of this category have revealed, however, that the head also contains large nonstrategic, overdemanding, underpaying customers that require high service and show little loyalty. These are well-known organizations that are notorious for demanding services beyond the point of economic return on investment and seldom hesitate to change suppliers over trivial cost differences. It takes a specially gifted organization to make any profit on these dragons. Data from the studies used for this book show that these heads often contain customers that generate no profit at all for the firm; in fact, many cause an out-of-pocket loss. Care must be exercised to evaluate the amount of overhead costs buried in the large volumes that are present, but there are very few organizations that do not include some dragon heads where, after all true cost allocation, the level of profits is negative for some of the biggest customers.

Moving to the body of the dragon, where studies reveal most of the real opportunity for profitable growth exists, the depiction shows the next 50 percent of the number of customers but just 30 percent of the total sales volume. In this B category are found high-margin customers, characterized by strong loyalty, a willingness to pay for special services, and an interest in partnering for long-term mutual advantage. A surprise finding in the analyses was that this category typically contained many distributors. It is in the body of the dragon that the real opportunities were found to exist for building future profitable revenue growth.

Moving to the lower portion of the dragon, the next category is the upper tail, where the wannabes exist. The illustration shows that the C area contains another 25 percent of the customers, accounting for only 10 percent of the sales volume. There are possible sleepers in the list that could become viable customers, but they have low advancement possibilities. Most organizations avoid taking a hard look in this area, despite the need to weed out the potential winners from drains on resources.

The final area is a target for elimination. The lower tail of the dragon contains about 25 percent of the customers but 5 percent or less of the sales volume. In this D area are the out-of-pocket losers. The cost of selling and serving generally exceeds the value of the orders placed by these customers. Organizations also often fail to exercise the discipline needed to weed out this category. Believing that there is no such thing as a bad order, they allow sales representatives to waste time soliciting business from these customers, waste further resources entering orders that do not cover the costs of processing, and compound the error by wasting accounting and administrative help keeping track of them.

A specific example will illustrate the point. Exhibit 4.4 is a set of dragon data for a particular manufacturing firm. This billion-dollar organization had 1,650 customers at the time of the study being illustrated. The top 50, or only 3 percent, of the total accounts represented 67 percent of the revenues (a very small-headed dragon). The next 200 customers represented 15 percent of the total number and 24 percent of the revenues. For this firm, the upper part of the dragon was clearly important and required little weeding to improve

EXHIBIT 4.4
Preliminary "Dragon" Data Analysis

Category	Percentage of Total Accounts	Percentage of Total Revenues
A Top 50	3	67
B Next 200	15	24
C Next 450	28	9
D Bottom 950	54	1

profitable growth opportunities. However, the bottom two categories revealed the need for immediate action. The upper tail contained 450 customers, or 28 percent of the total, but only 9 percent of the volume. The lower end of the tail contained 950 accounts, or 54 percent of the total, but only 1 percent of the volume. This firm had a bottom-heavy dragon that needed its tail trimmed.

When the CEO was confronted with the data, and the suggestion that eliminating 950 customers could have immediate, beneficial results to the firm's profits, the first reaction was disbelief. Considerable study of the information was needed before this executive could comprehend what had happened and then make the decision. An interesting phenomenon occurred when the edict was given to snip the lower tail and to weed out the upper tail. Many customers, when notified that the firm would have to discontinue supply, responded by asking the firm to continue supply—*at higher prices.* Many firms in the upper tail knew they had a good deal, and when exposed to the data revealing the loss to the supplying firm, they responded quickly by expressing appreciation for past performance and renegotiating prices and terms.

▶ A New View of Sourcing

Sourcing is the next area of concentration to be considered, but from a Level II perspective of how to support the targeted market, customers, and product. Now the firm begins working in earnest. Suppliers become crucial to the success of the strategy, but there must be a specific focus on how to apply joint resources. Putting aside the natural inclination to negotiate constantly for price concessions, both parties begin to realize there are more important uses for their time. The attention turns to how true partnering (a necessary precursor for Level III and IV activities) can improve the relationship. Longer-term positions are now bartered for beneficial ideas and process changes that bring savings to both firms. Alliances with the few key suppliers that directly affect most costs are considered, and global aspects might be brought into the discussions.

In Level II, the firm looks seriously at selectively outsourcing some activities to a supplier that can perform the function more efficiently. A firm that buys packaging, for example, might ask a key source to take over supplying all packaging materials, accepting responsibility for inventory but putting goods at the point of need in response to actual demand and not forecast. This latter necessity requires that the two firms exchange actual manufacturing schedules on a real-time basis. The relationship moves dramatically closer as previously sacrosanct information is passed between parties electronically, often using the same or compatible software. Only in this manner can a supplier hope to meet manufacturing needs without an enormous amount of safety stock. Next the two firms look at key partner alliances in which capital projects can save money for both parties.

> *The relationship moves dramatically closer as previously sacrosanct information is passed between parties electronically, often using the same or compatible software.*

In the most advanced stages of Level II, the partners look at how purchasing can be pooled to form larger buying entities. This pooling can take place across internal groups that do not traditionally cooperate or by forming buying groups with noncompeting firms. In the former case, the Tenneco Corporation sought help to form an internal pool that represented buyers from Newport News Shipyard, J. I. Case, Packaging Corporation of America, Tenneco Automotive Group, and Tenneco Gas, all subsidiary units of the parent holding company. In this arrangement, an analysis was made of the major purchases by each subsidiary. Steel became an early target because that was the number one purchased product. The list continued down through computers, software, copying machines, fax machines, paper products, and many other items. Using this list, one member of the pooled group was assigned to buy the commodity for the entire company. With this pooling, the leverage increased, and more attractive arrangements were negotiated. The time spent negotiating for these products was also reduced to a very small effort.

In the latter instance, where an external alliance is formed, non-competing groups have united to form a consortium, the purpose of which was to buy for members through one entity. Firms that are noncompetitors can develop alliances and dramatically reduce the cost of purchasing by having one representative, from one member organization, buy all of a particular commodity for all the other members. Paper, packaging, copying machines, computers, and other purchases can be pooled so that a single order-entry function coordinates many ship-to locations.

▶ Focus on Overlooked Areas

Pricing is one of the most neglected of the supply chain improvement opportunities. Believing that there cannot possibly be a complication in this area, many companies overlook it until they pursue Level II opportunities. The fact is that most organizations give away 2 to 5 percent of the selling price before the orders are processed. Even where sophisticated pricing systems were encountered, instances of poor pricing were discovered when a thorough assessment was made.

Discounts are the leading culprit. People in the field, dealing directly with the customers and intent on securing the orders, often interpret their responsibilities and negotiating freedom from widely differing views. As the orders are sent to what is usually a clerk, or at best a dedicated customer service representative, the opportunity for error and reconciliation is introduced. If a large order is entered and an extra discount is taken, the clerk can challenge the order, but the order generally moves forward in processing. Work with one major consumer goods firm revealed a minimum of one extra person per entry location, engaged in cleaning up errors in entry pricing and later reconciling inaccurate pricing. Further investigation showed a net loss in pricing of 3 percent to the firm.

Order-to-cash brings focus to how a business enters orders, makes something, gets it delivered, and gets paid for the effort. It is a process through which the firm examines how work is done from the point of customer contact to satisfactory delivery of products and services. It includes activities that cut across virtually every function in the business. Experience has taught that most Level II firms have a large opportunity for improvement in this sector of the business. Order entry is generally an overlooked area, with the result that too many errors are allowed to enter the system and be passed forward. By the time the data reach planning and scheduling, the need for manual interface accelerates, introducing substantial amounts of non-value-adding work. As the orders move toward order fulfillment, more instances of extraneous work are encountered. Old legacy computer systems are encountered, requiring downloading data from one piece of software so that a spreadsheet can be made and information can be uploaded into another software program. The chance for more errors at each interchange is a real problem.

Three areas are typical of the opportunities found in order-to-cash processes.

▸ *Inadequate fill rates.* Most organizations overrate their levels of satisfaction in this area. When customers are interviewed, the numbers are generally well below those being shown internally, but it is not unusual to find the top 20 percent of customers (those in the key category) receiving 80 to 90 percent of their orders completed as promised, when the demand is for 98 to 100 percent. The balance of the customers receive anywhere from 60 to 80 percent fill rate, when a minimum demand is for 80 percent or higher. Such conditions lead valued customers to seek competitive bids.

▸ *Higher-than-necessary inventories.* Due to the long order-to-delivery cycles in most systems and the low forecast accuracy, buffer stocks and safety goods are included throughout the supply chain, dragging inventory turns to single digits, when the leaders are approaching twenty-five to fifty turns per year.

▶ *Functionally centered process steps.* Due to a lack of integration across the order fulfillment process, the presence of segregated and individually managed process steps (order entry, planning, manufacturing, and distribution) opportunities are introduced for conflict and delays. A Level II organization takes the time to assess this process, from beginning to end, to determine how to build a flawless process, with reduced cycle times and greatly improved efficiencies. It does so to define the work activities one more time in a rigorous manner, but with a focus on identifying and satisfying customer needs, while vigorously challenging all non-value-adding activities. From this assessment will come the means to analyze, measure, and improve the overall business performance in a typically neglected area of concentration.

Exhibit 4.5 summarizes the benefits available if a firm takes the time to thoroughly analyze and improve the order-to-cash process. The chart shows that for a $1 billion firm, the opportunity exists to improve earnings by 30 percent. Beyond the direct savings potential, there are also major opportunities to improve customer satisfaction significantly.

▶ Enterprise Resource Planning: Connecting Orders to Delivery

Enterprise resource planning is a process that lies in the middle of order-to-cash, a process that enables an efficient and effective execution of the strategic plan by properly connecting orders (demand) to delivery (supply). ERP is a formal management technique that provides a single operating plan that links all business functions. Since ERP employs a single database for making decisions and operates continuously, it enables an orderly response to whatever demand exists and to the changes that are part of any operating system. The impacts on supply, demand, manufacturing, and inventory are considered across the entire business cycle and are reconciled from the most general to the most detailed level. When enacted properly,

> *The impacts on supply, demand, manufacturing, and inventory are considered across the entire business cycle and are reconciled from the most general to the most detailed level.*

EXHIBIT 4.5
Potential Benefits of Improving Order Fulfillment

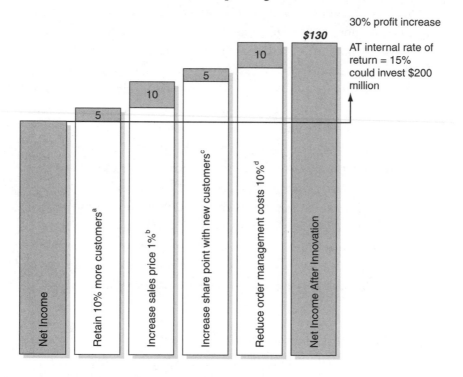

[a]Assume 50 percent of profits from repeat customers.
[b]Assume $1 million in revenues.
[c]Assume current share is 20 percent.
[d]Assume order fulfillment is 10 percent of sales.

ERP will yield significant measurable results and provide an ever-green financial plan for a regional or globally focused business. A large and growing body of software specialists is ready to help any Level II firm seeking advice in this area of supply chain management.

▶ Logistics: The Leading Component of Level II Progress

Throughout the studies conducted, *logistics* has been the leading improvement area in Level II firms. Significant research supported by the Council of Logistics Management (CLM) has provided a wealth of information and case studies for teams seeking advanced progress. Shipping is always the first area of concentration, as teams challenge the need to own and operate internal fleets. Effectiveness of the shipping function gets attention next, to make certain that equipment is being used to the best possible extent. Warehouse efficiency has become a major area of improvement as teams challenge the need for storing finished goods.

One of the largest food distributors in North America offers an example. This firm investigated its quarter-century-old distribution system and found that it could reduce its distribution centers from twenty-five to twelve while ensuring higher customer satisfaction. Using software designed specifically to analyze demands, flows, and logistic costs, the firm documented that it was simply paying for unnecessary assets. Other firms discovered they could consolidate their warehouses, in a pooled manner, with those of noncompetitors and accomplish greater efficiency. Procter & Gamble worked with key customers to eliminate a significant amount of its warehouse space by delivering directly to customer facilities.

Logistics still offers great promise as an area of opportunity, but a network study should be part of the analysis, and that requires a focus on external supply chain issues, a topic discussed in later chapters. Most Level II firms have improved shipping, warehousing, and distribution operations. What they need is the open thinking that allows the teams to begin discussion with external organizations to move logistics to the next plateau of improvement, where resources are pooled to optimize national and global patterns of supply.

▶ Electronic Interchange

Electronic commerce is important at Level II. With the improved forecast accuracy that can be developed, organizations find that their database can be mined to enhance the marketing and sales effort. This database always contains far more information than is used by the average firm. By digging out the data that apply to specific markets, customers, and products, a company can improve its sales force effectiveness. The modern sales force is given the tools to react, at the point of customer interaction, with information that can bring extra value to the customer. Knowing precisely what is available to promise thanks to accurate inventory information, an empowered sales agent can win orders that might otherwise be put out for bid. Using the more reliable and reduced cycle times, the sales rep can make promises that are better than the competition's and know that those promises will be kept. By providing access to the virtual inventory tracking system and to key customers within the segmented market structure, the customer becomes dependent on the more reliable system now available.

The leading Level II firms apply their resources to help customers plan and optimize promotional activities. Obsolete inventories become less common, and the promotions come into closer congruence with plans. Nontraditional markets can be attacked in concert with these key customers, as the data are now available to determine where the growth and profit opportunities exist and how the allied firms can pool resources to go after that business. Key customer alliances of a long-standing nature begin to blossom; they will be discussed as a key to further movement in Levels III and IV. Network selling now starts to appear as a feasible undertaking.

▶ The Opportunity List

The *focus* becomes more defined in this stage of the evolution, with emphasis on process redesign and systems improvement to optimize internal excellence. A major producer of consumer products for the weight control industry offers a specific example. This firm's Level II objective was to design and implement a new distribution channel strategy. The issues for this firm included significant erosion of share as new competitors were offering educational features and other purchase conveniences to consumers; drastically different order, ship, and billing characteristics of new channels; and the use of multiple food manufacturers to deliver products to grocery chains, a major outlet, and company-owned retail shops.

The team set out, with encouragement from senior management, to challenge every aspect of the existing distribution system. The first step was to build the process map and to apply an unconventional technique for this firm. At every step in the process, the team challenged the firm's core competency. That is, team members made a serious evaluation of the efficiency, effectiveness, and cost of the firm's performing the step versus having an external organization perform the step. Activity-based costing information was brought into play; every internal function was challenged to justify why the step should be kept in-house. Many trips were made to other firms and to external parties interested in outsourcing some of the steps in the process to validate the potential savings. The forecasting process was particularly taken to task to find ways to improve accuracy. A

> *A software solution was implemented, with the approval of customers equally interested in reducing the amount of inventory supporting the line of products being sold.*

software solution was implemented, with the approval of customers equally interested in reducing the amount of inventory supporting the line of products being sold.

The team went through three iterations of recommended improved processes. At each iteration, senior management was asked to review and criticize the proposed changes. Outside experts were brought into these sessions to offer their advice. At all times, the emphasis was on objectively evaluating the capability of the firm against that of external firms performing similar functions. The final refinement came from working sessions with key customers to determine how and how often stocks should be displayed, moved, or replenished in the retail outlets. These customers began to share information on store consumption that had previously been withheld from suppliers.

The solution that was accepted included a newly designed channel-specific distribution infrastructure. Features included third-party handling of small lots and low-turnover SKU items, more frequent store deliveries with smaller safety stocks and supporting inventory, flexible fulfillment systems based on better forecasting techniques, deployment of stocks and inventories more directly related to consumption data, and enhanced organizational characteristics with better responsibility alignment and accountability.

The results were impressive: $10 million to $12 million capital investment avoided, a 25 percent reduction in inventory, facilitated expansion from eighty to seven hundred stores, and $3 million to $5 million immediate profit improvement.

The *tools* will now contain extended benchmarking and demonstrated best-practice data that various teams have gathered from industry leaders. Many visits will be made to study other leading-edge organizations. Systems improvements will be analyzed and documented to determine the fit from one industry to another or from one company to another. Activity-based costing will be introduced to begin determining the costs to serve certain customers and market segments. This activity allows a greater degree of realism to be brought to the reported results and to single out areas of the supply chain that should be redesigned.

The *action area* expands from a few departments in the midsection of the organization to upper and lower levels in order to achieve greater overall participation in supply chain redesign. At the lower levels, the workers who perform the actual operations that result in supply chain delivery are brought into the process as agents of improvement. Using their superior knowledge of the actual steps in the processes, they are approached in a sincere manner, with some monetary incentive as their reward for participation. The typical result is an outpouring of useful suggestions that can enhance the methods and systems by which the supply chain is improved. The most advanced firms use some of these workers to go directly to the customers, to discuss their role in providing unparalleled service.

At the upper level, the business unit leaders and their direct reports start to interact more directly with the teams to bring a greater focus to the efforts and relate them directly to business performance. The objective is to bring the details of the business unit's strategic plan into focus so that the teams see the relationship between their work and the improved profits and services. Other than the areas mentioned as having a special status, all functions are scrutinized to determine whether improvement can enhance the entire supply chain. Process mapping becomes a rigorous tool for *guidance* of further development of internal improvement and information technology.

With this enlarged business interest, the *model* of choice becomes a form of intraenterprise diagram that defines the importance of a good hand-off between internal sectors of the business, so the enterprise delivers what has been promised to the downstream customers and consumers. The focus can then concentrate on areas of poor interchange, where mistakes and errors still exist, as well as on untapped opportunities for further internal improvement.

▶ Alliances and Results

In a step that will aid further progress, *alliances* are formed with select suppliers in an attempt to discover where cautious outsourcing to the best partner makes sense. This results in the supplier's assuming full responsibility for the supply, including shipping the correct materials to the point of need in the required quantities. Transportation is typically an area where many firms find third-party providers can assume the shipment responsibility more effectively.

Training now focuses on leadership skills as the scope expands beyond polishing internal competencies to determining how the total network concept can become a part of the company culture.

Results from a Level II effort move the savings to a higher plateau. Purchasing finds another 5 to 8 percent savings as nonprice features are introduced into the relationship that benefit the buyer. Logistics adds 3 to 5 percent in savings, and inventory decreases 5 to 10 percent. White-collar productivity improvement becomes significant and is measured in the elimination of full-time equivalents.

▶ Movement Versus Self-Improvement

The risk at Level II is that a firm may merely recycle its own efforts and not move forward to lead an industry. The emphasis becomes so strong on using the supply chain to reap cost savings and to develop state-of-the-art internal systems and procedures that the firm may lose sight of what the market is demanding. Some firms are so preoccupied with getting to higher levels of internal efficiency that they forget they are merely improving their ability to make products no longer in demand by the targeted market sector.

No firm is going to stop its effort at cost containment or at improving internal functions. However, a well-managed firm does not allow that focus to become such an obsession that it overlooks working with external parties to redefine how to go to market or how to position the firm with a network of suppliers and distributors to dominate a particular industry. Those considerations will be the subject of the following chapters.

 *Chapter 5*

The Wall Between Levels II and III

The firms that progress to Level II in the supply chain evolution find a way to improve processes that affect internal costs. Some establish better customer service measurements. Others create new revenues as a result of simplified and more effective systems. These same firms continue to work at supply chain improvement until they wring about as much savings as possible from the purchasing, or buy, side of the chain. They cut cycle times and reduce logistics costs and inventories to respectable levels. They then face a critical choice: Should we continue to pursue our internal improvement efforts and find new ways to contain costs? Or should we pursue the alliances that have been started with a few of our key suppliers and customers, to forge an externally oriented network that could give us a superior market advantage?

A company adopts the first course of action only at the peril of being passed by a competitor that chooses the second. Having studied hundreds of companies making progress toward supply chain excellence, I have arrived at one clear conclusion: the future belongs to the supply chain alliances that target specific markets and build the value networks that satisfy customers and consumers, using interactive technology as the key lever of success. It does not belong to firms acting independently, no matter how efficient they become at internal processing.

Most firms view their supply chains simply from a cost perspective—as another element of the business that must be controlled and constantly improved. Such an approach will lead to significant savings but not to a secure and prosperous future. Companies that optimize their full supply *network* find they can increase profitable revenue growth and enhance shareholder value by balancing cost containment, asset utilization, customer satisfaction, and effective top-line growth. The leaders do this through alliances that did not previously exist with their suppliers, distributors, and selected customers. In the process, they must move from an internal to an external view of the supply network. They can then work proactively to develop their value network as a source of advantage.

> *Companies that optimize their full supply network find they can increase profitable revenue growth and enhance shareholder value by balancing cost containment, asset utilization, customer satisfaction, and effective top-line growth.*

Successful firms discovered some time ago the need to focus on such factors as global market trends, evolving technologies, the needs of their customers and final consumers, and actions taken by competitors. They also augment this list by acknowledging that no single business entity can meet all market demands on a large scale. Global competition by nature forces a company to give at least as much management emphasis to external factors as to internal ones. Without such a balance, a company cannot grow and prosper in the twenty-first-century marketplace.

Unfortunately, most firms considered for the present analysis remain at Level II, focused mainly on internal supply chain improvements. In their ongoing attempts at maximizing internal measurements of operating performance, they may add dollars to the bottom line, but their narrow, myopic focus reaches a point of diminishing returns. Their management teams eventually grow weary of chasing the same types of internal improvements, and they lose momentum. Innovation gives way to complacency.

Trapped by their own inertia and unable or unwilling to generate the trust necessary to succeed with external partners, these Level II firms continue to pursue internal improvements that have little meaning to the final consumer.

Leading firms free their managers and staff from constant focus on internal concerns so that they can pursue truly meaningful improvements that strengthen ties with external partners and produce visible benefits for customers and ultimate consumers. The essence of this change is more dramatic than may appear on the surface. Too much time and energy spent on negotiations between internal service organizations and departmental functions might improve relations among departments and introduce more control features, but it detracts from the firm's ability to build a global enterprise that can keep pace with the leaders. At one major utility, the focus had been on internal departmental excellence for so long that the detail and complexity of its internal processes resulted in costs that were substantially higher than those of its more agile competitors. Excessive handling and control techniques were prevalent, adding no external value to the consumers of the supplied power. As a result, the company's decision-making and management actions had become sluggish.

Moving continuous improvement to the next level of achievement requires the type of focus demanded by Du Pont CEO Chad Holliday. In a memorandum to managers shortly after he assumed his leadership position, he stated, "Continuous reinvention and revitalization remains our mandate. *We must now take the bold steps necessary to further reduce internally focused work that restricts our speed of execution and external focus.* As we do this, we will aim for more of our people to get closer to the external and economic realities of our times." The directive is crucial to this chemical firm's leadership in its complex global marketplace. It speaks directly to the need for external focus in pursuing the highest possible levels of supply chain excellence.

Du Pont will work with suppliers and customers to understand the strategic importance of linked supply chain constituents, so there is a commonality to their business plans. Together, these constituents will then determine the needs of the integrated network, bringing raw materials through converters, distributors, and customers to consumers. Both Du Pont and its allied partners will translate those intentions and needs into executable operational processes and technologies that support the supply network. The overall purpose is to ensure that Du Pont and its partners will respond proactively to changing consumption patterns and dominate the chosen markets for many years.

▶ Formidable Obstacles

Exhibit 5.1 is a simple illustration of the gains that can be achieved as a firm progresses beyond preoccupation with internal improvements toward higher levels of supply chain excellence. The journey starts when most organizations stop accepting minor changes to current performance (usually in Level I) as "adequate." It was not unusual a decade ago for companies to be satisfied with bringing forward new budgets each year that contained a 3 to 5 percent improvement to key measures of performance—a form of creeping incrementalism. Those days ended when organizations vaulted over the "leave me alone" barrier and moved to a doubling of normal improvements. The tools used included such approaches as total quality management (TQM) and corrective action teams (CAT). These tools were applied to double the returns on organizational effort.

When these efforts maxed out in the late 1980s, management focused on capital appropriations, and the barrier to further progress shifted from "leave me alone" to "there aren't enough dollars." This lament was usually met in Level II. Most action teams began looking for new capital as the secret ingredient, when the supply of employee-generated suggestions began to dwindle. But there never was enough capital to bring a firm to optimization. Roger Smith learned this lesson after he spent $60 billion on automation projects at General Motors.

Business process reengineering (BPR) entered the picture as a major tool when teams vaulted a second wall to move the savings to

EXHIBIT 5.1
Potential Business Gains

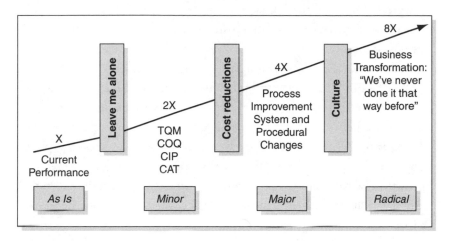

Note: TQM, total quality management; COQ, cost of quality; CIP, continuous improvement process; CAT, corrective action teams.

another doubling of results. Process improvement systems and procedural changes became the norm for making further gains. The focus that was later applied to the economic return on the new capital assets that were not providing the intended benefits brought a slowing to the large investments being made in the name of progress. New economic models now focus on return on capital invested, shattering many of the assumptions that prevailed in this era. Discovering that much of this capital investment was essentially wasted led the leaders into a new search.

What we now find is the final hurdle—a cultural barrier. It is the wall that blocks the firm from making the truly radical shift to an eightfold level of improvement, with or without major capital investment. This barrier is the real impediment to the third and fourth levels of supply chain management. Leaping over this barrier requires new thinking to counter the common resistance expressed in the statement "We've never done it that way before." The wall separating lower and higher levels of progress grows higher.

It requires strong leadership to leap over this wall, and most management groups, including many at the highest senior levels, will resist this final hurdle. In virtually every organization studied, there was a strong cultural resistance to moving to the external levels of progress. Those on the left side of the wall want to keep improving the internal mechanisms. Those on the right sense the importance of new demand creation and profitable growth (often in nontraditional market segments) through a stronger focus on external business partners, customers, and ultimate consumers. Firms willing to take this leap also see its critical connection with marketplace leadership and new sources and levels of revenue. In short, adding *shareholder value* becomes a key objective in the advanced stages of supply chain performance. Dramatic improvements in profitable revenue growth, asset utilization, and cost containment are fused into a single strategy that emphasizes customer satisfaction across a total network of supply.

Chad Holliday at Du Pont emphasized both the need for change and the technology connection when he told his managers in a memo, "We will grow as a company held together less by internal services and more by a focus on the *external* world. We will have much more cross-business synergy with our customers, technologies, governments, suppliers, and global external dynamics. This synergy will be created through modern techniques for networking across business lines including *use of the most effective information technology.* I will personally champion and lead the networking process to ensure that we gain more total power as a company."

That is the type of direction and sponsorship necessary to get over the wall separating Levels II and III of supply chain excellence. Anything less will keep the firm in Level II, since resources will remain focused on internal operational performance.

▶ Striking at Core Beliefs

There are two more levels in the supply chain progression, and the transition to the top must progress through the next stage of evolution. To reach Level III, the firm must vault over the wall that separates internal from external orientation. Many firms claim to have made that leap, but interviews with the individuals involved in driving the process reveal a different impression. In one multibillion-dollar manufacturing firm, many people in the organization were insisting to the CEO that the transition was complete when in fact all the emphasis was going toward gaining more capital for more equipment, thereby creating better internal efficiencies. Not a dollar was slated for joint investments with suppliers, nor were any resources targeted for network improvement with specific key customers.

Customers of this organization (as documented by later surveys) had reached the point where there was no distinction in the value of product or service being offered, and a majority of the key customers were searching for different sources of supply. Within the company, managers continued to discuss ways to apply more funds to gain greater manufacturing efficiency. The thinking was that this tactic would result in maximized profits, but no one bothered to read the telltale signals that the firm's customers were about to defect. The managers put continued improvements of internal performance measures well ahead of distinctive service capabilities and close attention to consumers' actual preferences. This firm has yet to make the leap to Level III.

Myopia must be eliminated to get over the wall, and many managers will be found incapable of the leap. A pilot project (described in Chapter 6) may be necessary for proving the validity of the advanced concepts to lead the laggards over the wall, unless the CEO is prepared to do it by edict (known colloquially as "a swift kick in the pants"). Along the way, there will be some senior executives who never make the transition. They simply do not understand what the external focus is all about. They maintain such an arrogant self-assurance that they make the perfect product or offer the best of a particular service and regard any customer who does not select their offering as either dimwitted or perverse. Because they deny the realities of their markets and resist a concept such as "intimate knowledge of customer preferences," they make it impossible for their company to move beyond Level II.

> *Myopia must be eliminated to get over the wall, and many managers will be found incapable of the leap.*

Getting over the wall requires a new business philosophy and a major change in the enabling supply chain processes. Along the way, the firm must shift its central focus to the consumer and to using the value network as a means of securing whatever loyalty is possible with those consumers who offer the most profitable future. The leaders willingly make the necessary effort because they know that it will result in greater control over both the supply and demand sides of the chain and will allow them to overcome shortcomings by one or more critical partners in that network. They view their company as an important link in a *value-chain constellation,* an organized network of firms working together by sharing resources and rewards in the pursuit of targeted markets and consumers. Thus they stand in sharp contrast to supply chain organizations that continue to focus myopically on wringing yet another dollar out of internal cost savings.

These constellations will supersede other, slower-to-adapt networks mired at Level II. They will use information technology as the major tool to find solutions to specific network needs rather than a cost to be continually reviewed and reduced. Such solutions will include computer-aided integrated marketing systems that seek critical new profitable revenues on a global basis. The most advanced will contain extranets linking supply chain constituents together in a low-cost, privileged communication system (described in Chapters 8 and 9). In these constellations, alliances will be formed with equally capable partners that achieve leading-edge performance in every area or sector of importance to that global growth.

As we proceed to the next two levels of progress, you must recognize the formidable barriers that often prevent firms from progressing beyond Levels I and II. The wall is high and broad. Overcoming it requires all the leadership skills a firm can muster.

 *Chapter 6*

Level III: Bringing the External World into Focus

To overcome the barrier separating Level II from Level III, a strong, dedicated leader is essential. This is not a task for a midlevel manager or even a senior departmental executive. The CEO or an officer in charge of a business unit, empowered to direct the journey, must lead the way using dedicated resources and the best possible talent.

Some champions have attempted to push their organizations over the wall by edict, levying grievous penalties for nonperformance or lack of cooperation. Progress using such a draconian approach, however, is usually short-lived, and companies managed this way remain at Level I or II. A skilled leader prefers to start with a pilot project in a single business unit managed by an executive who shares the leader's vision. When that unit's pilot project proves the value of working in partnership with external firms, and particularly when measurable benefits are observed, other business units take notice. In this chapter, we will consider in detail the leadership requirements and proof-of-concept pilot program that are essential for reaching Level III.

▶ Understanding the Value Chain Constellation

Exhibit 6.1 illustrates the next wave of supply chain optimization beyond a focus on improvements within the firm itself. At Levels I and II, where most firms are solidly situated, the emphasis continues on some form of reengineering and internal (intraenterprise) improvement. So long as opportunities remain to simplify operations and processes and to remove non-value-adding work, this reengineering will continue. The results will be positive but cannot by themselves lead to Level III.

It is important to understand, however, that progress to Level III does not mean a complete abandonment of efforts to improve internal operations, systems, and processes. Rather, the focus should now be on *integrating* these improvements with plans and actions aimed at creating a sustainable network of internal and external partners who are mutually dedicated to adding value for the ultimate consumer. The guiding concept is simple: no single firm can match the achievement of a network of organizations dedicated to cooperatively serving its chosen market.

In Level III, the goal is to redesign the entire supply network to establish *value chain constellations,* groups of interrelated firms dedicated to focused industries and markets. These constellations will

EXHIBIT 6.1
Supply Chain Optimization: The Next Wave

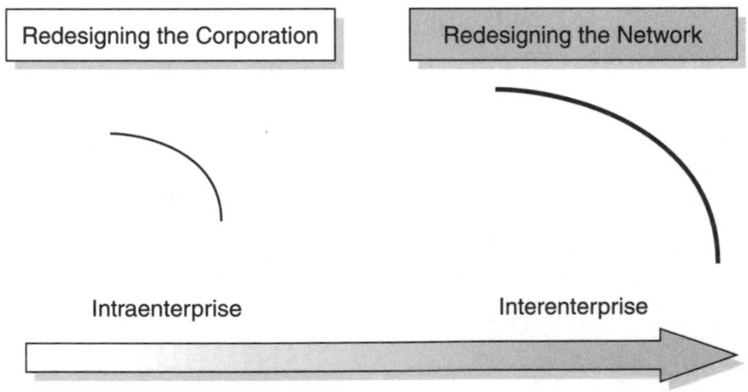

Redesigning the Corporation	Redesigning the Network
Intraenterprise	Interenterprise

pool their resources to establish a competitive advantage. A particular constellation will use these resources to redesign the entire supply network, starting with the most basic raw materials and ending when the final product has been consumed. Only when the driving force behind the interconnected activities is so focused and oriented toward network excellence will such an advantage be secured. And only when new levels of trust and cooperation are created in an interactive corporate environment—one transcending the traditional preoccupation with win-or-lose results—can such a constellation be established and flourish.

In the future, it will be the value chain constellation that finds the way to combine the supply chain improvements, gained by the linked constituents, into a system that most effectively meets the needs of the future consumers (many of whom are unknown at the time the combined effort begins). Success belongs to the best value chain constellations, not individual corporations. A business currently succeeding at Levels I and II may find this concept difficult to accept. As we will see, however, companies that do embrace the idea—those that have made a successful transition not only in their operations but also in their business philosophy—are poised for success at the higher levels of supply chain management in the coming decades.

> *Success belongs to the best value chain constellations, not individual corporations.*

To illustrate the benefits of a Level III perspective for a company that has traditionally focused on internal management, consider the paper manufacturer illustrated in Exhibit 6.2, a consumer products firm that had sustained a successful continuous improvement effort that yielded substantial documented cost savings for over five years. The firm had reached the point, however, where it suspected it had exhausted such internal improvement efforts as a source of significant further savings. In its quest for more savings, the firm turned its attention externally and found willing helpers from its list of key suppliers and customers.

This manufacturer developed a "rationalized network" that would offer a smaller number of products to the markets and customers deemed significant for the future, soliciting the external help of key

EXHIBIT 6.2
Case Study: Consumer Products Manufacturer

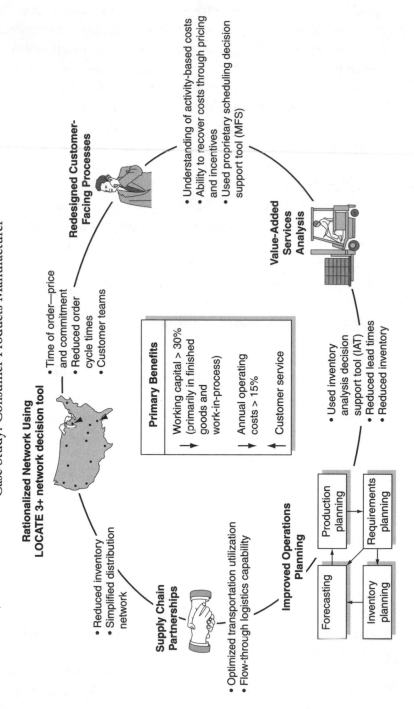

Rationalized Network Using LOCATE 3+ network decision tool

- Time of order—price and commitment
- Reduced order cycle times
- Customer teams

Redesigned Customer-Facing Processes

- Understanding of activity-based costs
- Ability to recover costs through pricing and incentives
- Used proprietary scheduling decision support tool (MFS)

Value-Added Services Analysis

- Used inventory analysis decision support tool (IAT)
- Reduced lead times
- Reduced inventory

Improved Operations Planning

- Forecasting
- Production planning
- Requirements planning
- Inventory planning

Supply Chain Partnerships

- Reduced inventory
- Simplified distribution network

- Optimized transportation utilization
- Flow-through logistics capability

Primary Benefits

Working capital > 30% (primarily in finished goods and work-in-process)

Annual operating costs > 15%

Customer service

customers and suppliers. The effort began with a thorough analysis to assess which of its major customers would survive into the next decade and have dominant positions with consumers deemed to be important for the company's future. Next the company examined the corporate cultures, business strategies, and past successes of these firms. Management tried hard not to let emotional bonds with long-time customers affect the objectivity of the analysis. The purpose was to select a small core group of key companies (future survivors) that would offer opportunities where the corporate cultures would mesh well, trust and mutual sharing could develop, and leading-edge technology would be the catalyst for success. An invitation was eventually extended to two of these customers to participate in a pilot project aimed at defining a more effective supply chain network, focused on specific end consumers of importance to both parties. The selected customers quickly responded affirmatively, and a pilot was arranged.

Work began with teams staffed by all firms and a professional facilitator to assess and develop prioritized opportunities to improve the total supply network. Cycle times and order-price systems became early targets. In another early step, the customer-facing process (the systems whereby sales and service representatives responded to specific customer needs) was redesigned for simplified, error-free transactions. The team quickly asked for help from the joint financial functions to provide cost information that would define the amount of extra costs in the customer-facing process and to develop an order-of-magnitude savings potential that would be shared among the firms. Making promotions work more effectively was an early area of concentration because it was obvious that such efforts were having little effect on annual sales or profits.

One team designed a new system for developing the promotions, using flexible manufacturing techniques to keep the supply chain stocked with the right amount of product in the stores where the promotions were having the best success. A special feature was having an ethnic variety of the limited product offering, to appeal to local tastes in areas where consumers of particular cultural backgrounds were buying the products. The same team also tested new products, including a particularly successful recycled paper product.

Recognizing a need for critical supplies to interface with the new delivery systems being developed, the firms then worked together to select a few key suppliers upstream of the paper products manufacturer. The objective was to further refine the network systems, particularly to cut cycle times by better coping with bottlenecks that had been identified in the first stages of the analysis. Three suppliers were asked to analyze the process flow from incoming material through store replenishment. For example, printing was an important aspect to identifying and promoting the finished product, so the most important supplier of printing materials was selected as part of the constellation. Activity-based costing techniques were applied to arrive at the true cost of supply chain transactions. Time frames and costs were added to each step in the process map to illustrate where the cycle was being unnecessarily extended and where the cost-to-value chain was losing position against competitive products.

One supplier provided very important data from an internal study conducted concurrently with the manufacturer's effort, but with a noncompeting company. These data showed the way to cut inventory needs and cycle time by interactively linking data systems. Operations planning was dramatically improved as the firms connected their computer systems and began an on-line exchange of replenishment needs from the stores and the inventory available from the suppliers. The customers were particularly cooperative as they fed actual store consumption data back through the system, all the way to the suppliers. In an unprecedented move, the three groups combined employees from their information technology groups into a special team to design an expanded information system (a shared intranet). The identified costs and gaps between current levels and benchmarks were then jointly analyzed; the goal to share savings provided an incentive to find solutions. The swift movement of data over the intranet considerably shortened the time from team recommendation to field testing and analysis of results.

As the relationship progressed and the joint teams developed higher levels of trust, value-added services (direct store shipment of "hot" items, diverted deliveries of needed stocks, help with stocking and display of product, scheduling changes to help any member of the constellation, and so forth) became an area of focus. The teams searched for ways to help one another, to streamline the flow from manufacturing to customer, and to better serve the customer's stores. This last effort required that the teams work directly in several stores. Representatives from the suppliers, manufacturer, and customer went together into the stores and worked with employees, interviewed consumers, and tried novel schemes to help consumers with the buying process and assist store personnel with the selling and promotion process. One result of this effort was to eliminate products that added little value in the eyes of the consumer.

> *Representatives from the suppliers, manufacturer, and customer went together into the stores and worked with employees, interviewed consumers, and tried novel schemes to help consumers with the buying process and assist store personnel with the selling and promotion process.*

Forecasting, transportation, and logistics activities approached optimal performance as the linked computer systems began working less with forecasts and more from actual store consumption data. The supply chain partnering progressed even further as the joint teams documented the benefits of their mutual efforts and leaders recognized their performance. Inventory turns rose significantly when the simplified network interactions moved the needed goods more effectively with far less safety stock. The network recorded a reduction in working capital of over 30 percent, and annual operating costs declined more than 15 percent. Ultimately, all parties realized that a major benefit of their cooperation was improved service levels, and customer satisfaction was at an all-time high.

▶ Transition Leadership

With this type of cooperation, a firm is ready to attempt Level III. Let us review Exhibit 2.1 from Chapter 2 (reproduced here as Exhibit 6.3) to see where we stand.

The *driver* of the process must be a specific business unit leader. This is a crucial transition. If the CIO or a designated supply chain executive continues to push the process forward, the firm will become

EXHIBIT 6.3
Level III: Network Construction

	Internal		External	
	Sourcing and Logistics I	Internal Excellence II	Network Construction III	Industry Leadership IV
Driver	VP sourcing (under pressure)	CIO/supply chain leader	Business unit leaders	Management team
Benefits	Leveraged savings	Prioritized improvements across network	Best partner performance	Network advantage, profitable revenue
Focus	Inventory, logistics, freight, order fulfillment	Process redesign, system improvement	Forecasting, planning, customer services, interenterprise	Consumer, network
Tools	Teaming, functional excellence	Benchmarks, best practice, activity-based costing	Metrics, database mining, electronic commerce	Intranet, Internet, virtual information systems
Action Area	Midlevel organization	Expanded levels	Total organization	Full enterprise
Guidance	Cost data, success funding	Process mapping	Advanced cost models, differentiating processes	Demand-supply linkage
Model	None	Supply chain—intraenterprise	Interenterprise	Global market
Alliances	Supplier consolidation	Best partner	Formal alliances	Joint ventures
Training	Team	Leadership	Partnering	Network processing

more skilled at those internal practices already improved, but it will not establish a network advantage in the eyes of the targeted customers or ultimate consumers. A specific business unit has to take the reins of control and bring an external focus to bear on what will be the beginnings of building the value chain constellation. The business unit leader should be someone who can seize the opportunity to use the supply chain as a vehicle for customer satisfaction and increasing shareholder value. He or she should be looking for ways to find improvements and savings otherwise passed over in the linkage of relationships across the total supply network.

Such a leader must understand and communicate the vision of an enhanced value chain constellation, identify the potential members, and work tirelessly as the architect of the ensuing network. The leader will see that additional benefits, something of greater value, can be generated through an external alliance of firms with common interests and dedication. The leader will understand the limitations of ongoing internal focus and the advantages of partnering with organizations focused on achieving the best possible performance at every critical link in the supply chain. This leader will foster the open discussion and apply the resources necessary to discover and set in place the most capable constellation of organizations to secure the future. With that network, the firm can pursue new markets and customers by offering products and services that have the best chances for success.

▶ Building a Cooperative Infrastructure

Nothing provides the necessary impetus for progressing to Level III better than solid results from a pilot test. In these tests, *benefits* beyond those attained by a successful Level II organization, gained through the involvement of outside firms, prove the validity of the concept and excite other business units to get involved. To establish such benefits requires a new type of infrastructure in which the best partner, internally or externally, is identified and takes responsibility for critical elements in the supply chain. This requirement strikes solidly at the traditional orientation of most large businesses. As firms grow in size, the temptation to build powerful internal networks, rather than best-practice units, becomes increasingly difficult to overcome. Firms with successful track records tend to establish stronger and stronger walls separating them from outside influence. These walls are cemented with the political aspirations that seem to come with size and dictate that all ideas of value have to be generated within the function or business unit. This cultural weakness must be addressed before the firm attempts to vault the wall separating it from outsiders.

The success of the journey hinges on an organization's ability to build an infrastructure capable of sharing resources in a meaningful

> *The success of the journey hinges on an organization's ability to build an infrastructure capable of sharing resources in a meaningful way.*

way. In such a situation, internal and external suppliers and customers join in focusing on products and services required to meet emerging market and consumer needs. They concentrate on the use of resources instead of protecting the interests of well-positioned political forces among the corporate elite. In some of the largest automobile companies, lack of an external focus has for years limited the helping hand that suppliers could have given to the automakers in their quest for greater safety and efficiency.

Several important business realities drive the necessary transition as firms realize that the old political model will not work in the future. First among these realities is global consolidation. In nearly every industry—particularly consumer goods, banking, retail sales, energy, and healthcare—mergers and acquisitions are accelerating the pace at which global multinational firms are securing market shares. As the players in a field shrink, the pressure for increasing operating efficiencies, reducing costs, and gaining a competitive advantage accelerates. These consolidations are forcing new relationships between suppliers and customers. For example, many food product manufacturers now find that twenty to twenty-five top customers could control over half of the annual revenues, and an equal number of key suppliers could deliver almost half of the cost of goods sold. Such strong leverage is not an unusual result of Level II practices.

These conditions can drive two reactions. The first and most traditional response is for a company to display its arrogance by insisting that the key suppliers submit to the buyer's model of operation and that selling and marketing strategies remain focused on moving products and services forward in the traditional manner. However, some companies follow a better alternative. Rather than view this trend as a threat, the wise company begins building the necessary alliances with external organizations so that mutual benefit is the logical result of continuing the relationships. They embark on this quest before the consolidation trend rules out potential alliances with the most advanced suppliers and customers.

These firms begin with a selected group of key suppliers, identified through early cooperation in Level II as crucial to the manufacturing and conversion process and having a compatible culture and future business plan. With this group, planning sessions are arranged (such as the partnering diagnostic laboratory) to begin preparing a joint process flow map and to identify ways the supply chain, serving mutually selected customers, can be dramatically improved.

A second response is the development of nontraditional marketing and distribution channels. Vehicles that were little more than concepts a few years ago have emerged as the channel of choice for moving large volumes of goods to selected consumers. The Internet and electronic catalogs are developing at exponential rates. Superstore channels now dominate some industries; examples include such retailers as Staples, Office Depot, Toys R Us, Circuit City, The Pet Store, and Home Depot—new channels that have altered business relations in the represented industries.

The ultimate consumers of some products and services have become far more knowledgeable and sophisticated in their shopping habits. They demand the perception of newness, greater value, and increased application of information technology. The staff's knowledge becomes critical to responding to those demands, and a shift in recruiting and training has enabled the superstores mentioned to provide the channel of response. Home Depot takes time to find employees for various departments who have actual experience in the area of focus. (How novel to have an experienced plumber help a do-it-yourself homeowner with plumbing needs!) With their success comes strong leverage over a supply base that is now positioned to bring larger volumes to one central buying location. Leading firms anticipate this change of position and move quickly to build a new set of relationships to ensure profitable transactions in the future. As they build their new models of response, alliances are secured along the chain of supply to eliminate weak links that could jeopardize the desired seamless flow of delivery.

With technology progressing at a frenetic pace, companies are being forced to rethink how they accommodate the computer-oriented consumer. Entire retail industries may soon be challenged to sustain their customer base. Lester Thurow, the noted futurist and lecturer, predicted in a speech delivered in June 1997, "In five years, we will have all the technology needed to close all retail stores." His point is that entirely new concepts of shopping are possible, and the enabling technology is already in progress. What is required is the vision to determine how to turn this trend into an advantage for a supply network that ends with retail consumption. Certainly, suppliers and manufacturers linked with some of the large retailers who lack a valid vision for the future are putting themselves at risk.

In such a dynamic and confusing environment, the ultimate success for suppliers, manufacturers, distributors, and retailers rests on their ability to cooperate in helping the network of supply survive and become the channel of choice. Adversarial relationships and arrogant dominance of the interactions are becoming increasingly unacceptable. Customers can no longer be viewed merely as conduits for moving products and services that enhance the profits of manufacturer or service provider but should instead be considered valued partners. Suppliers can no longer be viewed as necessary evils for providing the means by which the final products and services are created. The most capable external partners have to be selected and endowed with the responsibility to take over their link in the chain of supply, even if that means a dramatic shift in the organizational infrastructure. In conditions of cooperation for mutual benefit, arrogance has no place. Instead, a company must leave behind its traditional battle for individual dominance and pursue the creation of a value chain constellation.

When the leading customers near the end of the supply chain continue to build critical mass and secure the coveted positions with tomorrow's consumer base, they eventually realize their leverage. As they aggressively seek increasing differentiation from competitors, they pursue cost containment, asset utilization, and the building of more effective business systems. Assisting in the achievement of these needs is beyond the capability of most traditional sales organizations. The new leaders in creating customer value are building their skills in order to respond to what they view as a new set of customer needs, as well as a means of differentiating themselves among these emerging global leaders. The message is clear: leaders want to build alliances with organizations of equal capability, or firms that are as far along the evolutionary continuum as they are.

As a result of these trends, the win-or-lose battleground of the past is giving way to a more enlightened search for what James W. Gardner, senior partner at CSC Weston Group, calls "a symbiotic relationship between supplier and customer, in which each one's strategic agenda can be realized." As Gardner aptly points out, "In those circumstances where the objectives of the supplier can be blended with those of the customer, value is created and success is achieved." Under these circumstances, benefits are generated for both parties, far beyond what could have been achieved by the parties acting individually.

> *The message is clear: leaders want to build alliances with organizations of equal capability, or firms that are as far along the evolutionary continuum as they are.*

▶ A New Relationship Model

For most manufacturers and suppliers, the move to this type of relationship will require a transformation of the existing business model, accomplished via a four-phase process that involves (1) assessment of the current situation and strategies, (2) designing new processes and a controlling business model, (3) proving the concept through a pilot demonstration, and (4) implementing the new model in test markets or with test customers. Exhibit 6.4 describes these four steps as phases in project development.

In *Phase 1,* a manufacturer (or service provider) and a supplier of choice come together to conduct a complete assessment of their

EXHIBIT 6.4
Transforming the Business Model for Customer Leadership

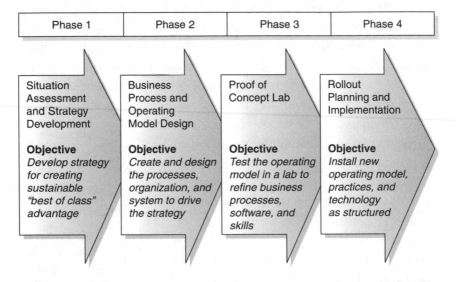

mutual business environment. This exercise includes internal and external evaluation of specific market and customer needs and what is required to meet or exceed performance by competitors. This work is conducted by cross-functional and cross-organizational teams, including the leaders and some outside expertise, to ensure that all aspects of the emerging model are identified and evaluated. This type of detailed approach provides a full perspective of the customer-supplier relationship and results in identification of customer value propositions that become fused in the developing value chain constellation.

Conclusions from the assessment generate clear imperatives for the relationship. A strategy consistent with the business plans and the mutual needs of the firms in the alliance emerges from these sessions. Action steps for going forward are defined, and mutual resources are assigned to progress through the next phases. Exhibit 6.5 shows a representative action plan that could result from the first phase of the effort.

In *Phase 2*, the strategic blueprint is used to move the designated teams into a design mode. Cross-functional teams are again used to

EXHIBIT 6.5
Realignment Action Plan

Strategy	Key Actions	Priority Initiatives
Build business by creating value for customers	Design and implement new promotion process	• Revise annual planning process • Create promotion evaluation process
	Establish control over costs	• Revise distribution system • Activity-based costing • Value-based logistics bundles
	Organize and deploy around strategic customers	• Customer teams • Account-specific resourcing
	Install efficient systems, technology, and tools	• Sales automation • Sales communication • Customer profitability

develop the customer-focused processes needed to execute the strategy and to define the pitfalls to be overcome and cultural changes needed to sustain positive results. Subteams focus on each key action in the strategy as the pilot model begins to take shape. This work generally helps identify the integration of efforts and systems involvement. The growing interdependence among the teams highlights the need for timely information exchange, and this need is met by an information technology team.

In *Phase 3,* the teams set in place the mechanisms for piloting their recommendations. The objective is to analyze the operating model in a laboratory situation for sixty to ninety days, during which the revised processes are tested for reliability and improved efficiency. Adjustments are made during this phase in order for the model to meet the demands of various business units. The real value of these lab sessions is that they bring together employees from the business unit that will be held responsible for implementing the new processes with systems designers in a real-time, problem-solving environment. Responsibilities for supply, levels of inventory, and deliveries are defined and resolved under test conditions that replicate actual business conditions, but with a small-scale risk to the organizations. Access to on-line information can be tested. How to use the data effectively can be proven, or systems can be changed to be more operationally friendly. The focus is not on individual or departmental heroics but on team results. Accepting team recommendations is not assured, however, as most organizations are used to applying functional expertise. Trials may be necessary to gain acceptance.

Finally, in *Phase 4,* the new approach and operating model are installed in a particular customer environment and tested under actual business conditions. This step can progress through a lead account pilot in which one particular customer is selected for implementation. One retailer, for example, could agree to allow the model to be implemented for a 90- to 120-day period in a group of stores in one geographical cluster. With success, the pilot could then be extended to a larger or even national rollout, after the process has been thoroughly tested and the feedback is used to fine-tune the model.

> *With success, the pilot could then be extended to a larger or even national rollout, after the process has been thoroughly tested and the feedback is used to fine-tune the model.*

A pilot of this nature is a major undertaking involving a serious commitment of time and resources. The amount of money involved is small by comparison to major capital projects, but the level of commitment is significant. Done correctly, such a pilot delivers the proof of concept that helps inspire the skeptics, and its *benefits* far outweigh the costs. More important, it becomes a giant step forward in creating the type of relationships that are demanded for a transition to Level III.

Exhibit 6.6 illustrates some of the areas where benefits can be achieved at Level III when organizations come together to realign their joint processes to gain a market advantage. After such an exercise, most participants agree they have been involved in a win-win situation, and an opportunity has been created to develop a competitive model that will enhance future business opportunities.

For example, a major white paper manufacturer went searching for improvements to its order fulfillment process. Following action meetings with suppliers and customers, a pilot was arranged in which

EXHIBIT 6.6
Typical Results of a Realignment Process

- Identification of key customer needs (both demand and supply) and their importance and satisfaction
- Segmentation of customers by value—volume, profit, and strategic direction
- Analysis to determine highly leverageable needs (both supply and demand)
- Channel and geometric analysis
- Baseline assessment of supplier performance

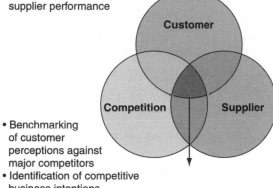

- Identification of internal barriers and issues
- Assessment of attitudes about customers
- Assessment of strategic alignment
- Comparison versus new customer-required capabilities
- Deployment of resources versus customer opportunities
- Process and organization period assessment
- Assessment of information technology capability

- Benchmarking of customer perceptions against major competitors
- Identification of competitive business intentions
- Assessment of performance in specific customer-related programs
- Establishment of best practices

a joint team investigated the fulfillment process, with special emphasis on work-in-process and finished goods inventory and how customer service could be improved while reducing operating costs and the carrying cost of safety stocks.

Process recommendations that came from this team effort included all of the following.

▶ *A new operational forecasting system, based on actual consumption rather than historical information.* The customers agreed to link up with the manufacturer's intranet and feed actual sales data by store. This data, it was agreed, could be shared with selected suppliers whose operations have a direct impact on delivery times and inventory levels to meet customer demand.

▶ *A new tactical planning and block scheduling process that met the needs of key customers and was transmitted in real time to suppliers.* The key customers gained a complete view of previously secret manufacturing schedules and now had access to these blocks on a preferential basis, so they could lower safety stocks held because of the unreliability of the previous system of supply.

▶ *Manufacturing process control limits that reduced the need for safety stocks to be held by the manufacturer.* With the interactive, on-line system, the need for these stocks for emergency shipment to key customers diminished, so the manufacturer also cut inventory.

▶ *Postponement of product differentiation to operations at the regional service center.* Most of the key customers wanted their own brand name on the finished product. This practice used to require the holding of custom-printed goods. The revised system included sending generic supplies to the service center for final printing of the customer name on an as-needed basis. The required inventory went from many with specific names to one on which the name was printed before final shipment.

The projected savings from this joint effort included a $2 million to $3 million reduction in safety stock inventory, a $3 million to $4 million reduction in cycle stock inventory, and a $2 million to $3 million reduction in finished goods inventory. All of these results were accomplished while increasing on-time delivery performance and fill rates.

▶ Leveraging the Supply Chain

As the move beyond the separating wall continues, a pilot group of organizations, joined in a tentative constellation, now brings greater *focus* on leveraging their new operating model and their jointly applied resources for the purpose of building profitable revenue growth. Cost containment and improved asset utilization are achieved, but the real proof lies in generating future revenues and higher profits that derive from the process redesigns and the enhanced working relationships created in Level III. Rather than merely transferring costs from one supply chain participant to another, the new model helps all network partners earn greater profits and competitive position by better meeting the demands of targeted ultimate consumers.

Exhibit 6.7 outlines the traditional choices for firms stuck at Level II. Depending on the internal culture, most organizations pursue one

EXHIBIT 6.7
The Drive for Profitable Revenue Growth

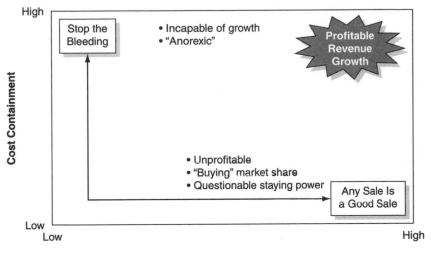

axis on the chart to resolve their business issues. The common strategy is to pursue cost reduction or revenue growth, regardless of long-term consequences. Either approach makes long-term *profitable* revenue growth an elusive target.

The usual result of a strategy focused on cost containment is an anorexic organization with limited growth potential. A study performed on eight hundred companies by the Mercer Company in the 1980s showed that 145 used cost cutting to achieve profit levels above industry averages, which was the trend of the time. A later study showed that only 34 of the 145 companies used revenue growth "as the catalyst for above-average profits by 1995." With constant emphasis on cost containment and headcount reduction, a firm runs the risk of losing the flexibility required by today's markets. Incremental amounts can be shaved from the operating costs, but increased costs for servicing and expediting usually offset those benefits. The result is no real growth in spite of the well-advertised headcount elimination and cost-control techniques.

Exhibit 6.8 highlights the fallacy of the concept on a larger scale. After laying off eleven thousand employees and cutting research and development spending by up to 50 percent, Scott Paper realized a

EXHIBIT 6.8
Results of Shrinking Company Size: An Example

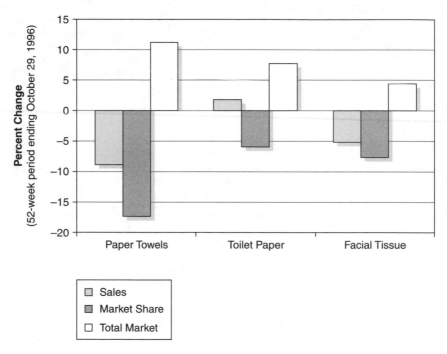

temporary increase in shareholder value, but it paid a relatively high price for this gain: its growth prospects were severely diminished. In fact, market shares declined in three major categories of business following these cost-cutting activities. The final result was the sale of this well-established organization to its rival, Kimberly-Clark.

Conversely, a corporate culture dictating that there is no such thing as a bad sale (the horizontal axis in Exhibit 6.7) will send a sales force in search of every possible order. As a result, the company will build unprofitable relationships that consume valuable energy that should go into strengthening relationships with key customers. Firms that make the types of market, customer, and product segmentation changes suggested in Chapter 4 find that their account list contains many of these energy-draining, unproductive relationships.

In another dramatic example of a national-scale organization, Exhibit 6.9 illustrates what happened when short-term pressures were

EXHIBIT 6.9
Proof That "Any Sale Is a Good Sale" Can Be Fatal

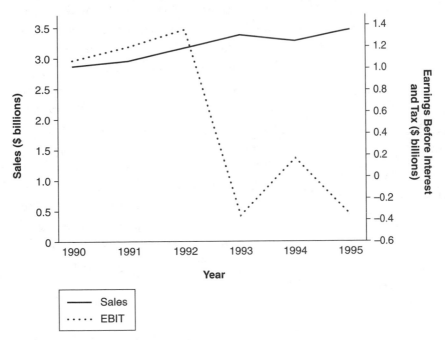

brought to bear on Kmart for increasing sales at all costs. Under an edict to raise store sales, revenues rose from the period 1990 to 1995, but earnings before interest and tax (EBIT) declined dramatically. Obviously, there was a serious flaw in thinking that all sales contain profit.

The path to profitable revenue growth must combine sensible elements of both strategies but should not be biased by intentions that detract from the central purpose. Traditional sales and marketing tools are not always able to provide the correct growth in mature markets. In the search for profits at any price, many firms have been misled by a reengineering focus that goes too deep in cutting costs. Cost containment is a necessary part of any mature business, but it is not a sustainable source of revenue or profit growth. "No company has ever shrunk its way to greatness" is a stark truism. At the same time, aggressive growth strategies pursued without understanding of the profit impact can fulfill short-term shareholder desires but is not always sustainable or profitable.

The obvious compromise is to pursue a course that goes at a diagonal across the chart in Exhibit 6.7, toward profitable revenue growth, sustained by appropriate costs and efficiencies and a focused selling strategy. A company does not abandon cost containment in this scenario but balances it to meet a well-designed revenue growth strategy. That strategy may in fact call for *increased* costs to provide personnel and other resources that support special initiatives aimed at securing long-term profitable growth and competitive advantage. The value chain constellations being formed by Level III firms are bringing their focus to this type of orientation. The concept is simple: build joint business strategies around consumers and markets that will provide the kind of return necessary for future reinvestment and sustained growth. That is the essence of a value chain constellation—a network of alliances jointly dedicated to future viability.

> *The concept is simple: build joint business strategies around consumers and markets that will provide the kind of return necessary for future reinvestment and sustained growth.*

With a coherent strategy designed around the network of relationships, the linked firms can make promises that would be highly speculative for loosely affiliated alliances. One chemical firm that has moved into Level III can show customers, over its extranet communication system, exactly how much product is available to promise (ATP) on a global basis, because the interconnected suppliers are joined in a virtual supply chain of inventory that ensures that quantities indicated on the ATP listing are real and in place. That network can chase backward, to the primary source, any critical material or chemical necessary for delivering the finished products to the interested customer.

Building a long-term, competitive advantage and sustaining market leadership requires that the constellation capitalize on this type of network strength. This means, among other things, error-free transactions accomplished over an interenterprise electronic commerce system. That system has to be faster and more reliable than any competing network. Availability to promise finished products and services is accomplished on-line, paperwork is at a minimum, and the benefits to all parties are clearly recognized. Under such conditions, the partners begin to approach optimization internally and externally and thereby create a unique market advantage.

A portion of the profits from this new arrangement is set aside to reward helpful participants and to reinvest without creating a huge debt-servicing cost. The mission will be changed from an internal-only focus for the constituents, and the organizations (or at least the driving business units) will be looking outside for future gains. The supply chain will contribute to each party's revenue growth, and savings gained along the way will finance further effort. Marketing and sales programs will be created in a joint fashion, with promotions tied to events that benefit the constellation.

Some of the direct improvements can be described as follows.

▶ *Promotions will be more targeted, specific, and controlled as initiatives that achieve specific sales growth.* Random promotions will be replaced by enhancements directed at specific consumers, customers, and time periods. The details of handling those promotions will be worked out in concert across the full supply chain, so the right amount of the right product is at the right place at the right time.

▶ *Price begins to disappear as a leverage point for gaining new business.* Margins are assured for all parties to the alliance, but costing is understood across the network (through full-value chain analysis), and additional savings are sought and shared by the constellation.

▶ *The network moves toward a "consumer-of-choice" franchise,* using the best possible internal capabilities across the constellation to meet the specific needs of the selected consumer base. That means the capabilities of the network are matched with the designated market, customer, and consumer characteristics so there are no weak links in delivering the right products and services to the end user.

▶ *A new level of trust among members of the alliance begins to emerge,* allowing the interacting firms to become comfortable with sharing resources and savings from their joint actions.

This set of conditions changes the old Level I and Level II models substantially. With the future markets and consumers of choice increasingly well defined, organizations are chasing the finite spending capacity within those segments. There is a limit to how much any segment can spend without falling hopelessly into debt and fiscal irresponsibility. This generally entails finding the way for one network to rob customers from other networks. Historically, this stolen growth arrives through aggressive pricing, comes at the expense of margins, and lasts only until the loser in the market warfare reacts with a counteroffensive. Such battling for share of market can be costly indeed, as cereal manufacturers found when the industry lost an estimated $1 billion during the 1996 "cereal wars."

A better alternative is to meet the demands of today's consumers for freshness, innovative selling techniques, and ready availability in an error-free environment. This condition is being met by a small but growing number of interconnected value chain constellations that understand that several organizational minds working in concert can beat one acting independently, no matter how large and experienced. These networks do not use price as the primary weapon but rather rely on value and service to secure new revenues.

At Level III, companies are using the following approaches to win in the marketplace:

▶ Going beyond forecasting models to defining demand via a connected web of information that feeds actual manufacturing schedules to the key suppliers, so reactions are based not on speculation but on current plans and schedules
▶ Dedicating the network to providing a level of customer service unmatched by any competing constellation
▶ Continuously working on the interenterprise relationships so that improvement moves from internal excellence to network excellence

These are characteristics that bring focus to the external world and define how a value chain constellation can gain a competitive advantage in selected markets for a specific consumer base. In the next chapter, we will complete the Level III scenario as we detail the balance of the influencing factors in the evolutionary stage labeled "network construction."

 *Chapter 7*

Joint Information

With a combination of organizational entities working in concert for profitable revenue growth, a new set of *tools* comes into being. Capital and other assets must be deployed efficiently and wisely across a whole network, not just a single business unit. Inventory, for example, must be considered a network asset used to ensure a seamless delivery of replacement orders and minimize fixed capital investment and obsolescence. In short, margins should be maintained across the network, or the alliance will falter.

A network flowchart shows the many steps contained in the value chain constellation. This chart must list the capacity constraints, the interfacility processing that takes place, the processing time at each step, and the yields and demand fluctuations. At all times, the network is driving for efficiency and customer satisfaction. When partners in the alliance analyze these flows, they realize the high value of data made available throughout the network. The joint databases can be mined to gather and share information on how to pursue the designated markets

113

and customers and how to build the supply of products and services that maximizes profitable revenues.

▶ Network-Oriented Actions

The network creates new metrics to measure the efficiency of the entire supply chain, not that of just one constituent. These metrics will include factors more important to the customer and consumer than the suppliers and manufacturers, such as number of stockouts, inventory availability, turnaround time on materials returned, order lead time, and customer satisfaction ratings. Forecasting takes a back seat to on-line interconnectivity showing consumption quantities in real time. Replenishment is measured against what has been pulled from the system. The planning process combines the strengths of the constituents to the value chain constellation so that parties no longer report what they *think* is available, what capacity *might* be used, or what they *could* expedite to meet demand. Rather, actual capacity is known across the network on a real-time basis. Orders are entered by a predetermined class of customer and product and fulfillment on an actual-need basis.

Master planning is done on a global basis using constraint-based loading to ensure that any promises made will be kept. (Software from companies such as Manugistics and i2 Technologies can be very helpful in this area.) All tactical issues are managed as though orders were crucial to the total system, not just to one supplier. Dependent demand materials are linked to the key suppliers who know as much about incoming demand as the firm that interfaces directly with the customer. Any complications are transmitted immediately across the entire enterprise. Diversion of supply can be made to accommodate emergency situations without disrupting supply through normal channels.

> *Master planning is done on a global basis using constraint-based loading to ensure that any promises made will be kept.*

The improved order fulfillment process provides such reliability that safety stocks are dramatically reduced and customers know they will get orders filled reliably and fast. Delivery is performed on short interval cycles with extremely high fill rates and on-time delivery percentages. These deliveries are not made on a "day of" basis but rather to a designated time slot at the customer's receiving dock. Unused assets have been removed from the infrastructure, and the value chain constellation is applying core competencies to ensure the most efficient processing (at least for the core products that make up a very high percentage of the new business). Exhibit 7.1 describes the type of interconnectivity implemented at Level III.

Under this system, demand information is fed electronically into the planning models for each constituent in the value chain constellation. Output from the planning models is used interactively to develop a virtual inventory that is the basis for a real-time, available-to-promise report. Orders are entered and transferred across the constellation without errors (through a redesigned process that requires fewer steps and thus minimizes the errors occurring at each hand-off). They are then fed to the scheduling models in a manner that not only sustains high fill rates and delivery integrity but also takes advantage of the available system capacity without wasting asset utilization. Strategic (long-term) planning uses a one-year horizon to allocate requirements to the various plant sites and to balance capacity with constraints.

EXHIBIT 7.1
Linking Supply with Demand

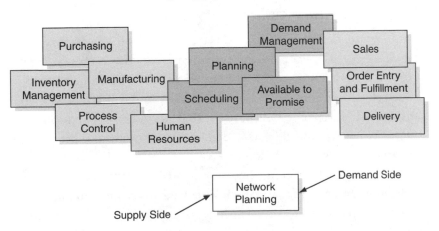

Product creation still comes through research and development, but the cycle time for movement of new products to market is optimized by having the best partner take responsibility for the crucial steps in the path from concept to commercialization. Human resource planning is also performed on a long-term basis with a focus on lowest unit cost, all the while making certain that the essential personnel are available and trained to ensure the appearance of a seamless supply to the consumer.

Actual production planning moves on a shorter cycle, typically four to six weeks, with a six-month horizon. Weekly loading profiles are generated for the planning of raw material needs and communicating with plant scheduling. A detailed, finite schedule is made for each site, providing adequate (but not excessive) inventory to meet incoming demand. The actual production window can be as low as hours but will fit the overall flow of processing and the sequence of operations. These schedules will be on-line, for access by all members of the alliance, and for making downstream schedules that interact properly with the incoming flow of materials and subassemblies. Simulation models are used to create "what if?" scenarios and to determine the cost effect from shifts in demand and supply. Global effects can be simulated for increases or decreases in inventory and production. A new tool that determines capacity value on the basis of dollars of margin per hour will be used to determine how to share capacity across product lines or to shift manufacturing between facilities.

Electronic commerce becomes a major tool as the alliance is linked ever more tightly together with current market conditions and with the consumers being courted. From initial sourcing through planning, manufacturing, and delivery, the parties in the alliance can track the flows toward the demand that is satisfied on a real-time basis. Selling techniques are expanded to take advantage of high-speed electronic communications. The sales representatives have an instantaneous real-time view of network flows to potential customers. (More information will be provided on the most advanced stages of electronic commerce in Chapter 9.)

A case study from Sun Microsystems will serve to illustrate how new information tools, particularly electronic ones, are enabling value chain constellations to succeed. John Blaine, vice president of supply management for Sun's worldwide operations, describes the company's experience as "making virtual reality." For this company, the effort expressed the vision of its chairman and CEO, Scott McNealy, who states, "At Sun, partnership is at the core of our business model. The right alliances can help influence gross margins, reduce costs, and allow us to focus on our core competencies. That's why we put so much emphasis into purchasing and supplier management, since this important function is a key part of our success formula."

Sun is a $9.0+ billion company that has worked hard at internal excellence to the point that its revenue per employee now exceeds $400,000, a record for the industry. Other metrics are impressive and show the value of the company's continuous improvement programs. The "virtual operations" effort began as an extension of internal progress, but with an intention to include external alliances. Sun was driven by a vision of the ability to link with customers and suppliers and leverage one another's core competencies to establish the best "route to the customer." Sun expected certain advantages from an extensive joint effort:

> *Sun was driven by a vision of the ability to link with customers and suppliers and leverage one another's core competencies to establish the best "route to the customer."*

- Seamless integration across the supply network
- Elimination of all redundancy
- Fostering an atmosphere of trust
- Developing the synergistic capabilities of the suppliers to the network
- Leveraging of each constituent's core competencies

To ensure a significant impact from the effort, Sun began with an analysis of current conditions. Fifty percent of purchases were concentrated with five key suppliers, representing 50 cents for every dollar of revenue. An early focus clearly had to be on strategic supply management with these suppliers. The components from this supply base included memory, mass storage, microprocessors, monitors, and external manufacturing. The total cost of ownership—or the cost to each constituent for its part of the processing aggregated to reach the total delivered cost—guided the development of the new virtual relationship. Joint problem solving became the major tool in developing the value chain constellation.

Strategy teams were developed and assigned to specific supply chain partner leadership. Guided by a three- to five-year view focusing on global impact, these cross-functional and cross-organizational teams went forth to produce a formally recognized portion of the product strategy process. To understand mutual interests, Sun meshed its own business strategy with suppliers' long-term objectives. Early in the effort it became clear that Sun was validating these mutual interests by making suppliers' R&D dollars work for the benefit of the total supply chain. A business process simplification project, as shown in Exhibit 7.2, was soon established to tap the best practices across the network.

Combining internal and external perspectives, Sun invited suppliers and customers to critique the process and make recommendations for improvement. Results from this effort were immediate. Cycle times went to all-time lows. Infrastructure cost was reduced as the parties with the best core competencies assumed responsibility for their part of the process. The number of days' sales outstanding shrank as the parties implemented electronic processing. Most important, a flexible systems infrastructure was introduced to support the ongoing business changes in a dynamic market. The traditional model of supply-to-manufacturer-to-customer was replaced with streamlined and integrated processes that worked backward from actual consumption, pulling products from a virtual supply system.

As a special feature of the effort, a "procure-to-pay" supplier council was created with the five key suppliers. Membership was at the presidential or vice presidential level, so a quasi–board of directors was set up as a think tank to improve the network further. This council introduced a revised corporate mission statement, titled "Vision 2001," intended to guide the future course of the seamless relationship and identify benefits to be realized by all supply chain partners. A separate product development vision was established to include suppliers and key customers in that process. The number of action teams eventually grew from the initial 10 in 1995 to 150 in 1997. Results included the following:

EXHIBIT 7.2
Business Process Simplification Project at Sun Microsystems

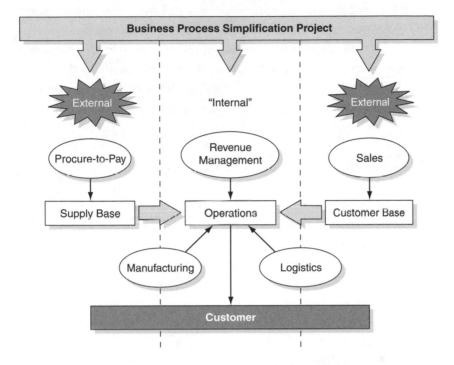

- Reduction of turnaround time on materials returned to the supplier from fifteen days to one day
- Reduction of lead time on demand pull from warehousing to four hours
- 80 percent reduction in total inventory
- Reduction of total lead time from three weeks to three days and then to one day
- 47 percent reduction in cycle time for direct shipment of product from the supplier to Sun customers
- 45 percent reduction in inventory for postponement configurations (keeping product generic until the last possible moment)
- Increase in inventory turns from five to fourteen, with weeks of supply dropping from ten to three and one-half
- Removal of five weeks from the cycle for real-time field quality feedback to the supplier

Sun is convinced that its pursuit of external alliances and efficiencies played a key role in its progress. The journey began with a defined vision in that direction, proceeded through joint efforts that had a major impact, and went on to establish lasting relationships of value to what is now considered "virtual operations" that ensure seamless product flow from the supplier through Sun and finally to the customer. Sun has become a Level III firm that has a value chain constellation headed toward dominance at the highest level of evolution.

▶ A Combined Action Area

The *action area* expands dramatically in Level III as symbiotic forces across the value constellation are released in cooperative pursuit of profitable revenues. The scale moves from favored departments and business segments to a global emphasis on how to capitalize on the total resources of the constellation, internally and externally. The action area becomes a global selling arena in which the combined powers and technology of a dedicated value chain constellation seek competitive advantages that secure the future.

Pressure to change the company culture intensifies in this area through the appearance of what is termed "defining moments." These are incidences that interrupt an existing pattern of behavior and create a need for a change from past practices. During these moments, superficial cooperation disappears as members of the allied organizations become traumatized over the prospect that things really are going to be different. They sense that the security of doing things the way they have always done them in the comfort of a large corporate atmosphere must vanish, to be replaced by a new cooperative response that involves external resources. More important, these moments result in an unsettling but necessary realization that an external party may be better at performing a key function in gaining new business than an internal group.

> *During these moments, superficial cooperation disappears as members of the allied organizations become traumatized over the prospect that things really are going to be different.*

There are three phases to these defining moments: *initiating, amplifying,* and *anchoring.* Each has a particular characteristic. In the *initiating* phase, the need to adjust to the new cooperative model demands that the current operating state be destabilized and redefined, which requires breaking existing patterns of behavior, most of which have been oriented around the win-or-lose situation that required one party to dominate the supply chain relationship. Once again, such changes are best tested under pilot conditions, rather than putting an entire organization under stress. These pilots will show the organizations the actions necessary to adopt a new corporate culture that fosters greater trust of external partners and resources.

During the *amplifying* phase, the situation is clarified through detailed examination of the pressures and reasons behind the changes required. For example, the need to use shared distribution facilities rather than the typically larger and individually owned sites is demonstrated through accurate performance metrics. This clarification reinforces the need for a shift in behavior, and the defining metrics make the exercise more public.

In the *anchoring* phase, the manner in which each person must perform his or her role and what constitutes acceptable behavior are made clear. The company announces a drive for consistent performance and begins tracking results. New job descriptions and management systems begin to filter into standard human resource documentation.

The key premises behind these defining moments are the following:

▶ They can be either a response to the new external opportunities or a reaction to breakdowns caused by reliance on the old cultural imperatives.
▶ The moments can derive from a new strategy or vision, a case for action initiated by a senior executive or the business unit champion, or a response to a competitive threat.
▶ These moments can create a need for further redesign of cooperative processes, based on actual results of the new alliances and test results of a pilot.
▶ A special moment can occur because of the need to create a new business alliance with another external party, found to be crucial to the competitive advantage being sought.

Leaders of the change process have to understand why it is necessary to create or respond to these defining moments and what these moments' potential impact will be on the interlinked organizations.

Returning to the three phases, that means that in the *initiating* phase, leaders must listen to the organization and understand the employees' reactions. They have to put aside their own cultural biases and reinforce the central purpose in creating the value chain constellation. They need to establish leadership credibility by making sure the culture adapts to the needs of the network. They have to demonstrate a sincere willingness to take calculated risks, without putting careers at risk, until the proof of the concept has been established and defining metrics are in place to measure performance.

In the *amplifying* phase, the leaders have to insist on consistency of statements and actions of the senior team members. They have to deliver reinforcing communications that support the need for cultural change. They have to create solid success stories that support the validity of the network.

In the *anchoring* phase, the leaders must confirm the actions being taken by the change agents and build the best new practices in the human resource systems (for example, job descriptions, organizational positions, and job responsibilities). They have to recognize and reward the desired behavior patterns and provide opportunities for others to create defining moments.

▶ Guidance Linked with Differentiation

With the value chain constellation defined and the need for changing cultures understood, the linked organizations work on strategic alignment. Recognizing the need to transcend the status quo, the teams pursue new business, armed with processes that will differentiate their network from competing alliances. Profitable revenue growth, asset utilization, cost containment, and greater customer satisfaction are the measurements of success, all of which will enhance the return on shareholder value for the participating firms. Innovative approaches to business will be under the *guidance* of leadership determined to link new practices and performance with superior business results across the constellation.

In reality, despite joint network strategies defined on paper, most organizations focus on a collection of individual functional strategies. These practices are refined over time within the limited range of thinking established by an internal focus. Gradually, the linked organizations begin to look beyond their own companies for opportunities to create and pursue mutual business strategies. In the process, the traditional model evolves through integration of individual business strategies into a coherent constellation strategy.

The objective of this new constellation is to improve the network's total business performance and generate greater economic return that enhances shareholder value across the network. The enabling characteristics will be the forging of new opportunities for growth, greater operating efficiencies, state-of-the-art (and beyond) information systems, and a seamless integration of the processes necessary to deliver value and service to ultimate consumers of choice. Done properly, this new alignment will not be in conflict with the business unit strategies but will complement them in a way that adds value to total organizational performance. Strategic imperatives that lead to the success of the total constellation will rise to the surface and, over time, subdue parochial concepts that benefit only a portion of the constellation.

> *Strategic imperatives that lead to the success of the total constellation will rise to the surface and, over time, subdue parochial concepts that benefit only a portion of the constellation.*

Advanced cost models will be important tools used by the allied firms to prove the validity of the savings and value to be gained through a cohesive, unified supply chain alliance. The need—and the opportunity—to differentiate the network will gain importance as the numbers generated by this deeper economic analysis show the major benefits of creating competitive advantage through innovative techniques.

Working together with the results of one or more pilot studies, the constellation will be guided by a tool such as the fusion leverage model depicted in Exhibit 7.3.

Beginning with a drive for profitable revenue growth, the network aligns itself to seek higher margins and more volume. Based on these objectives, the network establishes strategic imperatives that require

EXHIBIT 7.3
Fusion Leverage Model

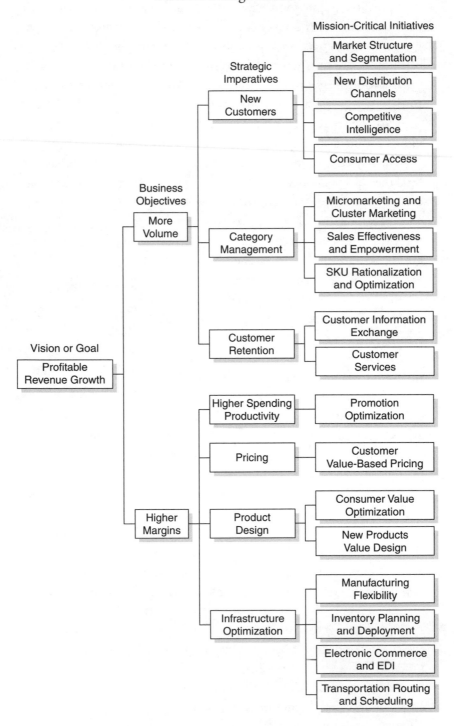

Mission-Critical Initiatives

Strategic Imperatives

New Customers
- Market Structure and Segmentation
- New Distribution Channels
- Competitive Intelligence
- Consumer Access

Business Objectives

More Volume

Category Management
- Micromarketing and Cluster Marketing
- Sales Effectiveness and Empowerment
- SKU Rationalization and Optimization

Customer Retention
- Customer Information Exchange
- Customer Services

Vision or Goal

Profitable Revenue Growth

Higher Margins

Higher Spending Productivity
- Promotion Optimization

Pricing
- Customer Value-Based Pricing

Product Design
- Consumer Value Optimization
- New Products Value Design

Infrastructure Optimization
- Manufacturing Flexibility
- Inventory Planning and Deployment
- Electronic Commerce and EDI
- Transportation Routing and Scheduling

cross-organizational cooperation and resources. Those listed in Exhibit 7.3 are some of the common initiatives pursued. Joint teams are then established to develop and prioritize mission-critical initiatives for implementation and to assign key resources to the action teams. The model will be fine-tuned as results are analyzed, but the network will always have some form of this model as a guidance mechanism.

In the pursuit of an aligned strategy and the means to implement the fusion leverage model, the members of the constellation will progress through four essential steps.

In *Step 1* (see Exhibit 7.4), team members come together to assess the scope and charter of what the constellation wants to accomplish. The objective in this step is to develop a preliminary business strategy. Using the multitude of data from their collective information systems, teams will consider the key suppliers, the focused customers, and the major competitors as factors affecting the integrated strategy they seek. Demand, supply, and systems considerations will converge into a framework for an integrated customer leadership strategy.

In *Step 2* (see Exhibit 7.5), the teams create the integrated model, focusing on a process-driven template that will apply now and in the

EXHIBIT 7.4
Step 1: Developing an Integrated Strategy

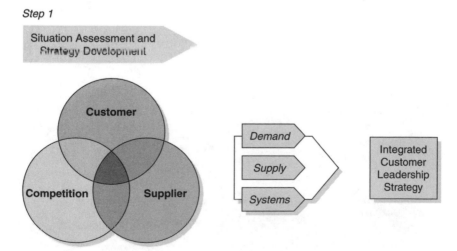

Step 1

Situation Assessment and
Strategy Development

Customer

Competition   Supplier

Demand

Supply

Systems

Integrated
Customer
Leadership
Strategy

future. Elements of the key suppliers' business plans are fused with those of the manufacturer and the intended customer. If distribution is entailed, the distributor's plan must also be considered. The purpose in this step is to define important enablers and how they will leverage strengths across the network. Capabilities and resources are used wisely to gain the best advantage. Reward and recognition systems are designed to add impetus to the effort. Technology and information are studied to ensure that the network has leading-edge capabilities.

In *Step 3* (see Exhibit 7.6), a core team is identified, driving the integration as implementation comes into focus. A subteam is designated to design the customer management and organization phase of what will become an experimental rollout. A marketing and promotion team is organized to design the support necessary for the effort, and a supply chain team is set up to make certain that all important elements differentiating the effort are in place at the time

EXHIBIT 7.5
Step 2: Creating an Integrated, Process-Driven Operating Model

Step 2

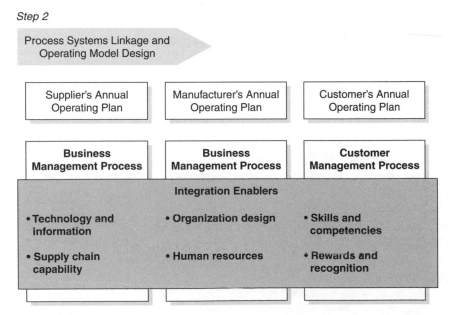

of the rollout. Information systems and technology aspects are considered across these team activities to support the quest for a market-leading position.

In *Step 4* (see Exhibit 7.7), an integrated operating plan is prepared for introduction into a test market. The teams now unite, using in-market experience to select the test market. A master plan and schedule are established with monitoring techniques to measure progress. Cross-functional and cross-organizational enrollment is arranged, and the effort is ready to go forward to prove the validity of the aligned strategy.

Armed with a leverage model and an aligned and focused strategy, the combined effort extends across the total franchise represented by the allied firms. Now the advanced costing information pinpoints where resources should be applied to make the greatest gains (which could be at any critical point across the network). Using the best partner to perform the required function, the vision focuses on optimizing

EXHIBIT 7.6
Step 3: Customer Leadership Process

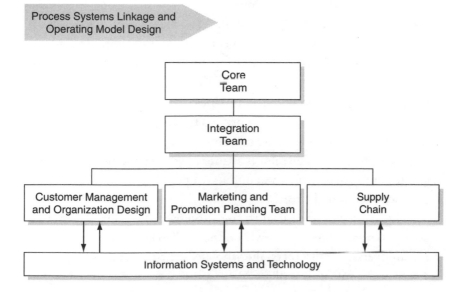

EXHIBIT 7.7
Step 4: Customer Leadership Output—
An Integrated Operating Plan

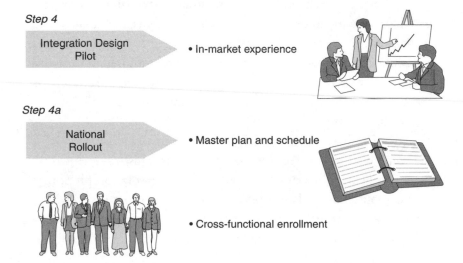

Step 4

Integration Design Pilot

• In-market experience

Step 4a

National Rollout

• Master plan and schedule

• Cross-functional enrollment

the entire supply chain. The pilot progresses under that orientation, taking time during the rollout to be certain to catalog the results, positive and negative, in order for the final model to be used as a template for furthering the effort.

The customer focus that was refined in the previous two levels of progress now takes on greater importance. A critical understanding comes into play: the cost of acquiring a new customer is many times greater than that of retaining an existing customer. Just as the network is trying to cultivate new business by luring dissatisfied customers away from another network, so the members of the network must be careful not to alienate customers integral to the created value chain constellation. The pilot is a time to verify possible animosities and to work collectively to define new operating relationships that enhance the mutual effort.

This issue will be crucial to the success of the pilot. Without a clear understanding of the newly defined collaboration between internal suppliers and customers, the whole effort fails. Leaders must take a very active role in this phase of the process to ensure that the best partner is performing the critical steps in the redesigned process and that transactions between parties are smooth and beneficial to the intended customer base.

Some of the important players will have a tendency to fall back into traditional positions, preferring to focus on continued improvement of internal processes and to protect their jobs. The team leaders must work diligently to eliminate this backsliding. The laggards must be shown the importance of supporting the new network strategy and new relationships with external partners. Supplier and buyer join in a critical link across the full constellation, and the consumer must perceive the entire flow of supply as uninterrupted. This requires all involved parties, who represent many organizations, to work flawlessly in a new environment of trust.

> *Supplier and buyer join in a critical link across the full constellation, and the consumer must perceive the entire flow of supply as uninterrupted.*

This condition will not come quickly or easily, and the pilot is the best way to determine what other actions are necessary to make the strategy work.

▶ The Interenterprise Model

The interenterprise model has been introduced previously to illustrate a straight-line progression from supply origin to delivery of the finished product or service to the ultimate consumer. As firms progress through Level III, that linear model must give way to a more circular model.

In Exhibit 7.8, the constituents of a value chain constellation are arrayed about the intended consumers of choice to the constellation who will decide from which network to make purchases. In this model, the linked businesses are operating collectively on a global scale to meet specific market needs in the sectors deemed most likely to provide the desired growth. A bidirectional flow of offerings (the marriage of products and services) that have meaning to the final consumer are delivered at each intersection of the model. A bidirectional flow of information—for planning, execution, and control systems—

EXHIBIT 7.8
The Aligned Interenterprise Model

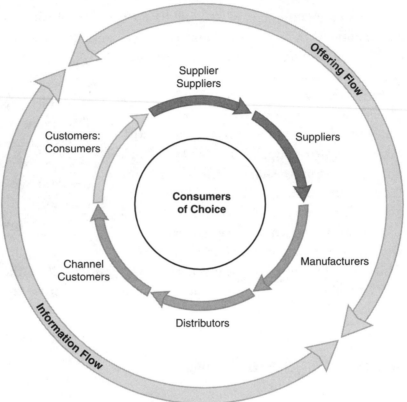

is in place to manage the operating processes, and a set of customized processes gives the constellation a significant marketplace advantage.

The benefits of the effort can now be truly realized because the constellation gains new revenues and returns on investment that would have eluded the partners working in isolation. The consumer benefits from the flow of innovative products and services, delivered at fair prices. The constituents of the network are making better earnings, particularly from the profitable revenue growth and shareholder value that has been enhanced across the total enterprise of interaction.

Many elements will come together as the *alliances* progress. Focusing on a small customer base that has great influence on the network, the constellation will apply cross-functional and cross-organizational resources to establish a solid go-to-market strategy that enhances relationships within the alliance. Quality products and services delivered through a competitively advantaged system will be meeting and exceeding the critical customer and consumer needs. Successful results of previous efforts will be combined to foster the use of best overall practices for network growth.

▶ An External View on Training

A new world of *training* beckons organizations with a vision of how external relationships can enhance future performance. As Level III value chain constellations are created, tested, and taken to market, an entirely new set of cross-functional and cross-organizational relationships will be established. At present, there is no training manual for how these very human transactions should take place and be enhanced.

We can do no more at this time than issue a call for action to training professionals to develop the kind of training that will enhance success. The individuals who direct the training effort for the various constituents of the value chain constellations should sit in on the pilot sessions, and as the teams build their aligned strategies, these professionals should determine the kind of complementary training necessary.

▶ Summary

Exhibit 7.9 illustrates the range of improvements that can be achieved at Level III. This chart reflects a study of two hundred companies identified as leading supply chain firms, not all of which would be classified as being in Level III. The organizations interviewed were asked what amount of improvement had been attained in the various categories indicated.

Work with the limited number of firms that have reached Level III confirms these results and serves as a guide for how much more

EXHIBIT 7.9
Best Practices from Actual Cases

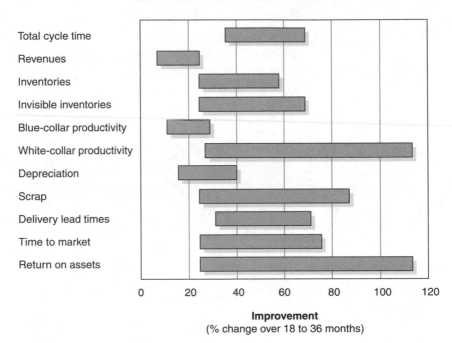

Improvement
(% change over 18 to 36 months)

is possible as organizations come together to combine their strengths and focus on specific markets, customers, and consumers. Supply chain management offers continued opportunities beyond those attained in Levels I and II. It requires a serious effort, however, to pass over the wall that separates the two sectors of progress. That effort must challenge long-held and firmly entrenched beliefs that all real progress is limited to improvements of internal functions and processes alone. The external world beckons, but genuine value chain constellations are being tested and pursued by only a few select firms. In considering Level IV, we will examine ways a company can progress to the highest plateau of supply chain excellence through powerful constellations that can dominate an entire industry.

 *Chapter 8*

Achieving a Vision for the Future

Moving to the fourth level of supply chain evolution requires the total involvement of all management teams across the entire network of supply. Progress occurs when team members realize that the supply chain offers a powerful means of competitive differentiation if they can transform their network vision into a value chain constellation that dominates their industry. There is no wall to vault over in this transition, just an extension of the mind-set that began in Level III. The driving force is the desire to be the first group of organizations to forge an industry-specific value chain constellation with a Level IV position. That force excites an individual management team and its allies because of the rewards available to the first network to become firmly established at the highest level of supply chain performance.

The constellation will reach this stage as a result of recognizing several keys to success:

▶ The venture must create new profitable revenues in order to secure management support.

▶ It must result in increased shareholder value to keep the stakeholders committed.

▶ It must establish long-term relationships with customers who will be the survivors and leaders in the future and who will serve future consumers, who determine the constellation of choice.

Effective use of network assets, sharing of resources, and continuous improvement are the catalysts. Shareholder value improves dramatically under conditions where the future revenue streams are secure and increasing with the most valued customers and costs are "prime"—kept close to competitive levels or slightly better. Those are the incentives needed to mobilize forces for one more push.

The essential ingredients of this final effort are imagination, determination, and technology. *Imagination* is required to see beyond the boundaries of "business as usual" and to build and maintain a strong external network that leverages the strengths of key suppliers and customers working for mutual success. *Determination* is needed to withstand the resistance that will come from many sources telling the leaders to withdraw into a more comfortable arena of self-preservation and to continue to focus investments on internal excellence. And enhanced use of *technology* is essential to keep pace with the tempo of business change on a global basis. This technology exists today; it does not need to be invented but does need to be adapted to serve the vision that leaders believe will secure the future and to establish advantages the network will have over competing entities.

> *The essential ingredients of this final effort are imagination, determination, and technology.*

▶ Matching Network Strengths with Customer Needs

To complete the final leg in the journey and translate the needed changes into day-to-day working guidelines, consider the following realities of today's and tomorrow's markets—considerations that deeply affect the demand side of the supply chain equation, for consumers and customers.

▶ Consumers have many choices, and they want to consider their purchase options easily and quickly determine that they will satisfy a need or desire at a fair price, without any quality complications. The value chain constellation satisfying those consumers must be prepared to deliver products and services that have value in consumers' eyes, return profit to the constituents (in order to continue investing in future offerings), attract customers most linked with the right consumers, and optimize overall results in the process. All of this should be done through a leading-edge communications system, with flawless internal technology ensuring the shortest possible response times.

▶ Consumers have become incredibly lazy. They want responsiveness and personal support when they have the slightest feeling of inadequacy, even when problems with the products or services are of their own doing. This requires that the network of supply meet consumer needs by solving any problems quickly and efficiently while representing the best interests of the firms in the constellation. Again, the need is for high-technology features that go beyond a responsive toll-free telephone service to an on-line electronic catalog of products and services that is easily interpreted and allows the browsing consumer to place orders or get service information quickly and accurately.

▶ From an industry customer perspective (the perspective of a manufacturer that supplies a retail customer or distributor), there is a demand for assistance from upstream constituents in building lasting business relations that enhance future viability. This condition requires that the network help the customers of choice build their business through assistance that differentiates these customers in the eyes of final consumers and increases their competitive capacity. These industrial customers, many of whom have become very sophisticated in electronic commerce and software implementation, require their suppliers to provide similar levels of sophistication. Winners in this game like to work with winners, not followers or pretenders. Therefore, the suppliers and distributors must bring the same level of technological expertise to the party as the manufacturers and retail customers.

▶ The total buying effect across the supply chain network results in a demand for innovative, effective, and efficient business systems. In other words, show me how to reduce my costs (from the customer perspective) or show me how to obtain values I will not get elsewhere (from the consumer's perspective), help me find better ways to get the sale, and prove to me that there is a competitive advantage in dealing with your network. Do all of this over an interenterprise connection (extranet) that is always on the leading edge, full of current innovations, and is simple and swift to employ.

These conditions require an integrated systems solution, not companies acting individually. That means that value chain constellation partners have to draw on mutual strengths to fashion the responses demanded by the new consumer population. These conditions are compounded by a growing generation of consumers hooked on electronic media, seeking a way to bypass traditional shopping mechanisms. For the customers of supply chains dealing with these consumers, any future system of interchange must contain elements of digital and electronic commerce. These elements will speed the cycles, eliminate work that does not add value to the system, provide the means for Web-based procurement, and introduce features for Web-based selling.

▶ Supply-Side Response

Switching to the supply side, there are conditions of response that should be met when a specific value chain constellation attempts the transition to Level IV. So few organizations have progressed to this point in their value chain constellations (Procter & Gamble, Wal-Mart, Toyota, and a few high-technology firms) that Level IV begins as a level playing field. Important alliances are still forming; value chain constellations remain in the developmental stages. Since individual firms alone cannot create the performance gap distinguishing their supply chain, the building of these network alliances is critical to a Level IV position.

To reach this level, the leadership groups of the allied members of the value chain constellation must work together to match supply with demand in a way that brings network advantage in a flawless and virtual manner to the targeted consumers. To do that, a number of actions are important.

▶ Given the need for quality and a variety of innovative products and services, there must be a transition from merely supplying quality products that work with marketing support to providing innovation, uniqueness, special sizes and assortments, financial options in the buying process, special services not offered by competing networks, and substantial attention to after-sale servicing. The goal is to ensure that end users recognize and act on the greater perceived value of the resulting product and service offering. This condition goes beyond having a "happy consumer." In fact, it results in an enterprise that so dazzles the consumer that he or she becomes a "customer for life" and will not even consider doing business with a competing network.

▶ With a demand for greater responsiveness and personal attention, the value chain constellation must move beyond focused account managers and specialized customer service representatives to virtual systems with on-line communication, cross-functional contacts, methodologies for quick problem elimination (versus today's emphasis on problem resolution), and an understanding of customer strategies. In addition, these systems must contain leading-edge communication networks that appear to be driven by persons and not machines. Automation is essential, but it cannot eliminate the need for personal attention or the feeling that a real person is part of the desired response. Anyone who doubts this fact should poll consumers on how they regard voice-mail systems encountered when requesting help from a supplier!

In addition, these systems must contain leading-edge communication networks that appear to be driven by persons and not machines.

Designing these highly automated, personally interactive systems is a real challenge for Level IV participants. Such an effort begins with a very special cross-organizational team focused on a particular consumer segment. This team then interviews those consumers to determine their perceived needs, buying patterns, and communication media of choice. Experiments with a few of those interviewed are then organized to test alternative virtual communication systems, designed to meet the consumer preferences. (This subject will be further discussed in Chapters 9 and 10.)

▶ The value chain constellation must progress beyond local market understanding and competitive knowledge to supporting the industry customers that serve consumers of choice. This help may take the form of strategic planning, useful data for business analysis, consumer and end-user demographics, marketing expertise in the focused arenas, financial modeling with solid costing information, and the means to measure network performance on a global basis. The supplier of tomorrow must be much more than a helpful ally. It must share the same vision and objectives, promote the same optimum use of key resources, and share the risk for making this last move in supply chain progression. Crucial to meeting this need will be the application of scarce and talented resources that go beyond providing internal help to assisting the value constellation.

▶ To react properly to the demand for effective and efficient business systems, the network must move beyond on-time, complete deliveries and accurate invoicing to activity-based costing to measure total system performance, to collaborative planning and virtual inventory management that bring a new high to inventory turns, electronic purchase order-to-payment methods, order status integration, and customized logistics services. In brief, the supply side must respond to the new demands with an impeccable state-of-the-art, technologically supported system that will take a competing network years to match.

To ensure that responses match needs, the value chain constellation will consider how to integrate a total systems effort that meets with market-driven opportunities while using the ultimate in high-technology equipment and systems. These opportunities are evaluated and the ingredients are matched with four additional areas that must be addressed.

Consumer opportunities that require nontraditional responses

Changes in the consumer segment that create new market dynamics demand alterations to methods of supply.

The key drivers of market segmentation that prioritize network response will change due to demographic dynamics (such as population aging).

The relevant past and likely future trends alter previous advantages and require new selling techniques.

Customer opportunities that alter methods of distribution

The emerging distribution channels of choice for tomorrow's consumers could require new alliances with new distributors.

The selling chain of choice in the consumer sector could require more emphasis on such emerging channels as offered by Web-based buying.

The interim customer relationships necessary during the transition could require more service personnel.

Constellation capabilities that determine the means of differentiation

The strengths and weaknesses of the current network compared to the changing scenario may require additional resources at key locations (for example, technical help with extranet communications).

The bases for potential advantage versus other emerging networks could require alterations to the network systems.

The matching of cultures and values among the constituents of the value chain constellation may require some discussion and fine-tuning of the action plans.

The profile of risk and how it will be shared among network partners will most likely require up-front negotiations and understanding.

Willingness to invest in the future together will need to be settled as further investment opportunities are met.

Requirements for continuous upgrading if the network is to sustain its advantage must be defined.

Competitive reaction that keeps the network alert

Key organizations and networks that are or could emerge as a threat have to be identified and monitored.

Current trends among other alliances in other industries that could be relevant should be tracked.

Basic economic conditions and changes that could hamper or enhance the chances of success must be evaluated by at least one member of the network and communicated to the constellation.

Potential barriers to sustaining the relationships of trust and mutual sharing of resources and benefits have to be evaluated and laid to rest.

An assessment of this type will lead to the identification of the advanced initiatives that will ensure future success. Specific criteria will emerge from the evaluation when the parties in the alliance begin to plot their future cooperative courses of action. In Level IV, the entity that began as a loose-knit alliance of partners intent on gaining a market advantage begins to coalesce as a formidable network of cooperation. Together, these partners take a collective look at just what will define the future matching of demand and supply in a manner far beyond what was necessary in the pre–Level IV stages.

▶ A Shared Vision

Hypotheses about future supply chain strategies will eventually define the model for Level IV actions. Qualitative research will be conducted among targeted end users so that necessary revisions can be made. The cross-organizational teams will seek innovative features regarding selling, display, order fulfillment, promotions, and other actions. The objective will be to breathe life into the hypothesized opportunities. Further tests and pilots will validate this model, and the value chain constellation will go forward to establish a competitive lead over any other constellation in the industry. The challenge is to define the model before any other group in the industry and thus to establish a dominant position.

To progress from Level III to Level IV, members of the value chain constellation must prepare a vision of future conditions so accurate, convincing, and forward-looking that it will inspire the collective bodies of the aligned organizations to cry out for action. This requires far more than mere pep talk—in fact, it must define the way an industry goes to market in the next century. The field is open, but the players are in training. The team that best defines the practices required to secure competitive advantage will be the team that leads in a particular industry. An appropriate vision will be detailed in Chapter 9 as we examine how a determined value chain constellation can create a galaxy of success.

> *To progress from Level III to Level IV, members of the value chain constellation must prepare a vision of future conditions so accurate, convincing, and forward-looking that it will inspire the collective bodies of the aligned organizations to cry out for action.*

▶ From Vision to Necessary Action

Currently, only a handful of value chain constellations are prepared for entry into Level IV. They consist mainly of large consumer or high-technology product manufacturers. They are doing all right, based on past performance, and their intention is to develop global supply networks with the characteristics described in earlier stages of progression, but there is still a tendency to make the final leg of the journey in an individualistic manner, bringing suppliers and distributors along only as necessary. Level IV is not the province of individual organizations, no matter how powerful, but rather of value chain constellations that have developed the trust and use of mutual resources that will benefit all constituencies. This means mastering a particularly difficult challenge: the sharing of resources and rewards.

A popular phrase from the movie *Field of Dreams* is "If you build it, they will come." For business, that entails building the supply network of the future now in order to have the first and best link with consumers. Customers will then patronize your value chain constellation and will stay with you.

An organization with a successful history built on very strong branded images or a superior technological gap over competitors will find it difficult, if not impossible, to share control over its total supply chain. Without a willingness to share, however, progress at the final level of supply chain performance will remain limited.

The best approach is to pursue a compromise position in which the strength of the brand is protected across the full supply network and the constituents have a stake in that protection. Companies that fit this category include Kraft Foods, Unilever, Intel, Anheuser-Busch, Hewlett-Packard, Heinz, Campbell's Soup, Gillette, Sun Microsystems, 3M, and Nestlé; all are in the process of building Level III and IV constellations, finding a model acceptable to the strength these firms bring with their branding. This model will be presented in Chapter 11.

The idea still begins by inviting a few key supply chain members to develop a vision together, focusing on protection of the strong branding position but also emphasizing the development of a seamless constellation that builds new revenues in nontraditional ways. Oreo cookies have such a strong position. That position must be protected, but Nabisco needs suppliers of ingredients and packaging, for example, to keep the brand at the forefront of consumption. Nabisco will never cede control of the process of manufacture and supply to any other entity, but it is well advised to work out tomorrow's network of supply with a few organizations capable of enhancing the possibilities of success. Such a move results not in abdication of control but rather in expanded opportunities for nurturing a mature brand on a global scale.

With a guiding vision worked out in concert with allies of choice, even the most powerful branded organizations will find they can improve their chances of future viability. With the right vision will come the actions necessary to secure such a position. The next chapter will elaborate on the development and enactment of such a vision. The final leg in the journey is about imagination, determination, and technology. Let us explore it together.

 *Chapter 9*

The Performance Gap

In Level IV, the impetus for success comes from collective management teams whose members realize the opportunity their joint supply chain network offers as a differentiating element in business marketing. If one organization is so important because of physical size or value of brands, this firm can be the "nucleus" constituent, but there must be network participation or else progress toward a truly powerful value chain constellation will fail. Membership on teams may also vary with the size and resources of the participating organization, but there must be team representation across every company's management.

These teams will create a network advantage that results in continued cost containment, better asset utilization, and greater customer satisfaction, and the firms will use this advantage to establish powerful new market positions. The value chain constellation will function with a strong consumer focus and emphasis on designated markets, customers, products, and services, generating new and profitable sales across the supply chain, often in nontraditional areas. The demand chain will be linked solidly with the supply chain in these networks, and the focus will reveal the areas of opportunity for significant new growth.

Exhibit 7.8, presented in Chapter 7, is a simple illustration of how a Level IV effort is guided. At this stage, the full network of interaction and designated consumer base must be clear, or there will be no real progress. The interactions, ready for final design, will be from initial suppliers to the final consumer. The extension of the network will be global, since multiple businesses will work together to meet market needs domestically and internationally. The flow of offerings is bidirectional, so it appears to the consumer as a seamless system that provides the desired products and services in the shortest time cycle and without defects in quality.

> *The demand chain will be linked solidly with the supply chain in these networks, and the focus will reveal the areas of opportunity for significant new growth.*

Another bidirectional flow of information supports the required functions in the system, with flawless interchanges. Greater accuracy and speed become tools of competitive advantage. A set of customized processes works in tandem with the effective delivery of goods and services to market. Today's technology is applied to ensure profitable revenues that would otherwise have gone to a more efficient network. The result is a set of leading initiatives for integrating supply chain activities across organizational boundaries and the development of a baseline performance model. That performance will add value for each constituent and result in unprecedented levels of consumer satisfaction.

▶ The Payoff: Higher Shareholder Value

In Level III, shareholder value begins to increase as the network begins to coalesce. In Level IV, the overall focus for the network constituents intensifies in ways to increase shareholder value for each member of the constellation. As this shareholder value increases, so does the payback for each stakeholder.

Exhibit 9.1 depicts factors influencing earnings and stock price. This illustration shows the stock price-earnings ratio as a function of growth and return on equity (ROE). Growth is affected by mergers, acquisitions, and organic or internal growth. Internal growth is affected by increased customer share, new products, and improved services. The highlighted factors in the exhibit are in the domain of supply chain management. With full cooperation across the network focused on the last two blocks in the growth portion of the diagram, significant synergistic effort can be brought to bear on new markets and customer bases. That is an arena of particular opportunity for the most advanced supply networks.

ROE equals profit before interest and taxes (PBIT) divided by the equity base. The numerator is affected by total revenues and annual costs. Cost containment is the traditional focus of supply chain management, and revenue is rapidly becoming a new feature. Less attention is given to the denominator. Equity is affected by investment of assets, both fixed and variable. These factors are a part of modern supply chain management efforts. Optimization is approached as cost effectiveness and growth are favorably affected, and fewer assets are used. In a thorough supply chain assessment, the employed assets are evaluated to determine where a network partner should operate the equipment, as well as in which plants and through which distribution centers the products should be processed. The goal is to eliminate unnecessary assets and use to best advantage those that satisfy consumer needs.

As the mechanisms for developing a Level IV position are detailed in this chapter, these levers for success will be highlighted as they are affected by external supply chain initiatives. We will consider how a network approach can make the best use of assets, fixed and variable; how increased customer share can be achieved with joint efforts focused on the right consumers; how new products and services can benefit from collaborative design and development; and how costs can be reduced through the dedication of joint resources to high-potential initiatives.

The aligned interenterprise model will be helpful in following the exposition, as there is still much confusion among would-be participants in value chain constellations regarding the best ways to integrate

EXHIBIT 9.1

Three Levers for Success: Growth, Assets, Costs

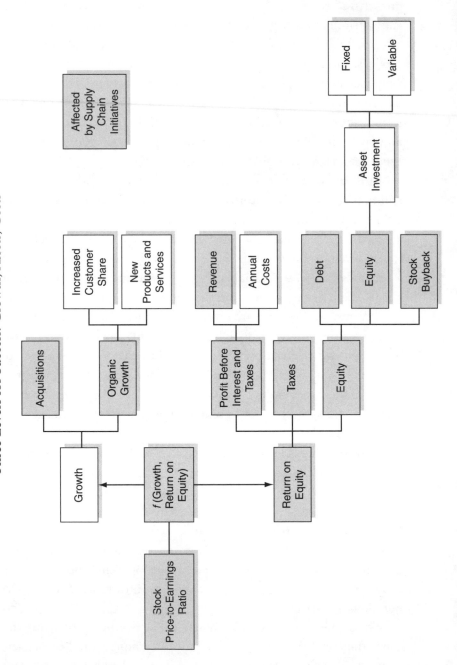

efforts. The actions taken are more often short-term and tactical than long-term and strategic. Because progress stalls for some would-be allies and relationships are not where they should be, significant value is not being added to the participating firms' margins. At this point, the faint of heart will give up the effort. They will neglect the opportunities offered by external partnering and thus miss a strategic source for adding shareholder value. Because tremendous cooperative effort is needed to make supply chain partnering a success, there is no substitute for a guiding model and metrics that report the savings for all parties.

As an example, consider the effects of supply and demand misalignment across a network that functions without the kind of cooperative efforts being prescribed.

In the typical commercial world, where pricing is the normal business-building strategy and margins can be razor-thin, capturing and sustaining market increases without resorting to price tactics is beneficial, even for the largest of competitors. The graph in Exhibit 9.2 illustrates the usual misalignments that occur between supply and demand as a product proceeds through its economic life cycle. As shown, demand is typically highest around the date of launch when supplies are elusive because the manufacturer is uncertain as to how well the introduction will proceed. During this period, distributors often tend to overorder as a way of hedging against shortages in the event the introduction is successful. Retailers follow the same strategy if they are impressed with the new product, creating excess channel fill, or phantom demand.

Because planning systems typically use previous-period demand to forecast future orders, this nebulous demand gets factored into forecasts, triggering a period of overproduction. In the interim, actual demand tends to taper off when imitations or competing products come into the market. Caught with returns, cancellations, and surplus safety stocks, manufacturers are normally forced to reduce prices to move the remaining stocks. Because of this price erosion near the end of the life cycle, distributors and retailers negotiate liberal price protection policies that shield them from losses by gaining a credit from the manufacturer for inventory still in the channel. Typically,

EXHIBIT 9.2
Supply and Demand Misalignment

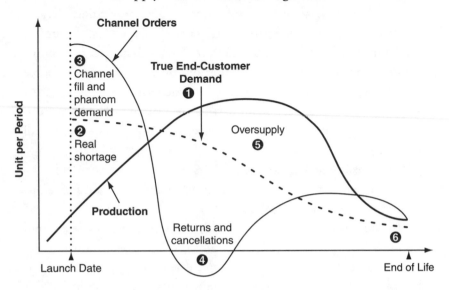

❶ True end-customer demand is unknown, must be anticipated.

❷ Production cannot meet initial projected demand, resulting in real shortages.

❸ Channel partners overorder in an attempt to meet demand and stock their shelves.

❹ As supply catches up with demand, orders are canceled or returned.

❺ Financial and production planning are not aligned with real demand; therefore, production continues.

❻ As demand declines, all parties attempt to drain inventory to prevent write-down.

the net result is so large that it becomes the greatest indirect cost for most manufacturers. Significant value is lost in the overall network by these hidden inventory costs.

Under a constellation approach, in which a networked structure functions to bring new products to market, the planning, scheduling, inventorying, and distribution processes are developed jointly. The result is closer coordination and far less reliance on safety stocks. Timing of the product life cycle is monitored on-line, with all parties accessing movements to the consumer. The virtual network of supply matches actual consumption much more closely, and forecasts become less relevant since all constituents are linked electronically and can plan from actual consumption. These pull systems match supply with actual demand, and the total network operates more optimally. When the product nears the end of its cycle, little, if any, inventory remains in the system because demand has been closely monitored. Given the global pressures driving down operating margins today, any network that increases cooperation among participants will provide greater opportunities for increased efficiency and maximized values. Under these circumstances, it becomes imperative for all constituents to explore the possibilities for further integrating their interorganizational activities.

> *The virtual network of supply matches actual consumption much more closely, and forecasts become less relevant since all constituents are linked electronically and can plan from actual consumption.*

▶ Connecting with the Consumer

The principal objective for the value chain constellation is to build enterprisewide solutions that harmonize the network activities into a system for satisfying the ultimate consumer. That technique ensures future revenues and sustained growth. It now becomes necessary for integrated solutions throughout the constellation, creating a need to align the business plans. The best tool for such alignment is to focus on interactive systems that establish a unique methodology for connecting with the final consumers, blocking potential competing networks that lack the electronic connections to the customers and consumers and cannot match the features of the new methodology.

The various corporate information systems (IS) strategies must be developed collaboratively and not in isolation. This need is becoming more apparent as supply chains move to higher levels of progress. A survey conducted by Computer Sciences Corporation (CSC) among 339 North American IS executives identified their top ten concerns (see Exhibit 9.3). The results showed that IS leaders are moving toward an external viewpoint as they relegate reengineering and internal improvements to lower positions on the list and give high priority to connectivity across the supply chain.

The CSC survey further documented that 62 percent of consumer goods suppliers had an Internet presence in 1997, compared to only 33 percent in 1996. It is apparent that the Internet has emerged as an important factor in the supply chain and is already changing the structure and interaction of markets and distribution channels. Organizations must see the Internet not as an option but as an essential communication channel among consumer, customer, distributor, manufacturer, and supplier. The business advantages are too significant to overlook. The Internet provides a standard, open

EXHIBIT 9.3
Top Ten Concerns of North American Information Systems Executives

Priority	Percentage of Managers Citing
1. Connecting to customer, suppliers, or partners electronically	81.5
Organizing and using data	81.5
3. Educating management on IT	70.4
4. Aligning IS and corporate goals	66.7
5. Integrating systems	59.3
6. Creating an information architecture	55.6
Improving the IS human resource	55.6
Instituting cross functional information systems	55.6
9. Implementing business reengineering	51.9
Restructuring IS	51.9

Source: Computer Sciences Corporation.

communication network that spans the globe, requiring relatively small investments and low operating costs. It can provide any information in a digital format to all who have the equipment required to access and use it. It is emerging as an essential tool for connecting value chain constellations and the consumers of choice. Internet features will be discussed at greater length when the tools of implementation are considered.

▶ Coupled Management Teams

As shown in Exhibit 9.4 (which reproduces Exhibit 2.1 from Chapter 2), when organizations progress to Level IV and pursue integrated services to consumers of choice, the *driver* must be the management team for the nucleus firm, in concert with key executives across the constellation. Ideally, various management teams will be combined to establish equal representation, but experience shows that this condition is rare. In most cases, one organization will have such a brand equity or dominant market position that its members will form the nucleus of the constellation, and suppliers, distributors, and customers will be arrayed around that nucleus. The driver then actually becomes a steering group, made up of senior members of the nucleus firm, with the help of other constituents.

For example, Du Pont might be at the center of a value chain constellation that includes raw material suppliers making up 75 to 80 percent of a business unit's cost of goods sold. One or two manufacturers that convert the Du Pont materials into a product such as carpet or clothing would be included, and one or two distributors and a retail customer that moves the final product to a select group of consumers would complete the constellation. Du Pont would host the initial meetings to design the supply chain and develop the charter and objectives. As the alliance progresses, other firms could become the host and take a greater role in the development of the network.

> *The value of well-known brands cannot be overlooked as constellation planning goes forward.*

The value of well-known brands cannot be overlooked as constellation planning goes forward. A firm with a stable of thoroughbred

EXHIBIT 9.4
Level IV: Industry Leadership

	Internal		External	
	Sourcing and Logistics I	Internal Excellence II	Network Construction III	Industry Leadership IV
Driver	VP sourcing (under pressure)	CIO/supply chain leader	Business unit leaders	Management team
Benefits	Leveraged savings	Prioritized improvements across network	Best partner performance	Network advantage, profitable revenue
Focus	Inventory, logistics, freight, order fulfillment	Process redesign, system improvement	Forecasting, planning, customer services, interenterprise	Consumer, network
Tools	Teaming, functional excellence	Benchmarks, best practice, activity-based costing	Metrics, database mining, electronic commerce	Intranet, Internet, virtual information systems
Action Area	Midlevel organization	Expanded levels	Total organization	Full enterprise
Guidance	Cost data, success funding	Process mapping	Advanced cost models, differentiating processes	Demand-supply linkage
Model	None	Supply chain—intraenterprise	Interenterprise	Global market
Alliances	Supplier consolidation	Best partner	Formal alliances	Joint ventures
Training	Team	Leadership	Partnering	Network processing

brands is going to protect its equity in those brands at all costs. Such an organization will bring a special perspective to the negotiations and will lead the way in determining how its brand is represented across the value chain constellation. In one well-publicized example, John Bryan, CEO of Sara Lee Corporation, raised eyebrows in September 1997 when he announced plans to divest Sara Lee's manufacturing facilities and focus primarily on the marketing and sales side of the business. As he considers turning the production of such well-known names as Sara Lee pastries, Hanes hosiery, Jimmy Dean sausage, and Kiwi shoe polish over to contract manufacturers, he is, in essence, planning to outsource all production.

This "deverticalization," as it is being called, brings a whole new dimension to the supply chain process, but it is consistent with the objectives of advanced supply chain management: arranging for critical processing actions to be performed by the best possible partner. In Sara Lee's case, senior management decided that because others in the network offer at least as much competency as found in the current internal manufacturing operations, these capable contractors can be trusted to perform this function. The nucleus organization can then concentrate on revenue growth, where Sara Lee adds the greatest value. Not insignificant is the $3 billion in cash that will be freed up by the changes.

▶ Adding Network Value

When the working arrangement is understood and functioning, the steering team focuses on adding value to the network. The guiding thesis is simple: the network is the new medium of consequence in business. Intrafirm communication systems must be logically expanded across the value chain constellation. Several specific agenda items quickly come into play.

▶ *It must be determined how to compress the supply chain organization and structure by identifying value-adding processes that may be unseen by separate constituents but could be performed by multiple firms. The goal is to eliminate overlap and redundancy by choosing the* most appropriate partner to perform the critical processes and to document ongoing improvement opportunities, particularly in distribution and inventory management. This action inevitably reveals duplication of effort and investment in inventories, paperwork, expediting, and other functions. It also reveals a significant amount of non-value-adding work and distortions in data exchange and processing.

The more autonomous the members of a chain remain, the more the transfer of information reflects cultural biases of the individual firms. In one example, working with a food converter and a major food distributor, we found agents working for both organizations, charging each for the same documentation on transactions and shipments. In another, it was discovered that one firm was placing extra orders to avoid stockouts. This group was falsely communicating to the network more demand than actually existed, thus triggering excess upstream supply in the system. This problem can be solved by measuring inventory inefficiency in the network and reconfiguring the total system for improvement.

> *The more autonomous the members of a chain remain, the more the transfer of information reflects cultural biases of the individual firms.*

▶ *Collaborative planning, which must be addressed immediately, allows supply chain partners to cooperate in structuring and executing the processes needed to bring a product from raw material sourcing to finished goods consumption as efficiently as possible.* It encompasses demand planning, order fulfillment, and capacity planning, with the best possible use of technology. Such planning offers rich opportunities to reduce the amount of raw materials, work in process, and finished goods in transit. Distortions created by poor input and processing of critical data result in costly overages, shortages, obsolescence, and expediting. The greater the amount of inventory dispersed throughout a network, the more difficult and costly it is to track these goods, make transfers, and keep the goods in prime selling condition to respond to current demand. Collaborative planning is the only means, short of constant communication, to bring efficiency to the network.

▶ *Collaborative planning begins by establishing the standards of performance that are critical to the customers and consumers and then pur-*

suing common actions that will meet these standards. The objective is to generate a more accurate demand signal for all the members of the value chain constellation. When better demand information is available, the next step is to synchronize order fulfillment, where joint decisions come into play on order size, frequency of shipment, ownership transfer, and other potentially controversial issues. In the optimal system, actual consumption drives replenishment. Joint capacity planning comes next, as the constituents try to use assets more effectively. This is a major opportunity that is often missed because supply chain partners are not aware of duplicate assets being underutilized. Return on those assets improves when the network determines which entity should perform which function. A crucial later step is determining how to share the gains among the constituents.

▶ *Products should be cooperatively designed to maximize the positive market response.* Although most integration activities in this area have been limited to specification and assembly help, true cooperative design goes well beyond such activities to leverage all partners' resources mutually as a tool for gaining powerful competitive advantage. Particularly for organizations interested in delaying final configuration—the so-called make-to-order or configure-to-order manufacturers—this technique is indispensable for success.

▶ *The partners must develop and implement technology that supports full and seamless collaboration.* Enterprise resource planning (ERP) systems are integrated software solutions that are essential to Level III success. For Level IV, ERP must be expanded to optimize the use of total constellation assets and capacity while ensuring high levels of efficient transformation from raw material to consumable products. At this level, ERP fully supports integrated, transaction-level processing by sharing a common set of data among all constituents.

Electronic data interchange (EDI) is yesterday's news. It is necessary for Level II success but is a relatively expensive system to apply on a network basis. Level IV requires a decision support system using intranet, Internet, and extranet technology to bring real-time, on-line capabilities to the constellation. The objective is to provide a highly efficient, seamless, and reliable flow of clean, useful data from the beginning to the end of chain. Electronic commerce (e-commerce) is the tool of choice today to support a full value chain constellation.

Nothing less will suffice for this highest level of supply chain performance. All three systems—intranet, Internet, and extranet—will be described in more detail when we consider the tools of implementation.

E-commerce involves the use of technology and communication networks to facilitate business-to-business and business-to-consumer transactions via the shortest and most accurate means. Done properly, e-commerce will result in significant improvement to service, revenue, and profits.

▶ Benefits from Nontraditional Areas

Benefits will come from the network advantage and the flow of new profitable revenues. Purchasing takes on a new meaning in this advanced stage. With most of the benefits already secured on the buy side of the equation, attention now turns, with the help of network partners, to the issue of strategic purchasing or value sourcing. A consortium approach is taken to purchasing similar items and commodities across the constellation. For example, a network designed to deliver clothing will have raw material suppliers that purchase cotton or wool from primary supply sources. These supplies are sent to manufacturers that transform the raw goods into fabric. Converters might take the fabric and turn it into shirts or slacks. A distributor could take these goods to retailers, who in turn sell the finished products to consumers.

Each constituent in this network may have worked diligently to minimize internal costs, greatly reducing the key supplier group responsible for a huge percentage of incoming costs. They may have also reduced warehousing and transportation costs but have not optimized certain items of indirect cost. Across the network, there are sources of less direct cost than cotton, wool, and dedicated conversion machinery. For example, each firm will pay for paper, copiers, computers, energy, telecommunications, janitorial services, contracted services, and maintenance. These costs historically come under less scrutiny. With a value chain network established, collective attention is given to reducing indirect costs by assigning responsibility to one person from each of the constituents for one cost category. Purchasing groups thus free up time formerly spent on negotiation and can now help manufacturing, design, and transportation functions work with suppliers to use all network assets more productively. In this way, the partners identify savings that would otherwise go unnoticed and realize that certain partners are especially suited to secure purchasing advantages that will benefit the entire value chain. A member of the purchasing group for the manufacturer, for example, might buy all of the packaging for the network, and another might buy all of the computers. Now the full leverage of the constellation comes into play. Measurable savings for buyer and supplier occur as a result of this approach.

Smart purchase cards and customized procurement systems in these advanced networks enable a total enterprisewide advantage, not just a temporary gain for one member. The impetus for further savings builds as these consortium buyers discover more and more nontraditional areas in which to demonstrate their buying acumen. By working with key suppliers over a longer planning horizon, valuable resources can be applied by both buyer and seller to work out special solutions, further reducing the total cost of transactions within the constellation.

Exhibit 9.5 illustrates the direction in which e-commerce is progressing for advanced sourcing techniques. From a central location, direct linkages are established with the key suppliers (this can be as far upstream in the network as makes sense for the value chain constellation). Electronic catalogs can be used for much of the nondirect materials and services required. Parts, subassemblies, and special services can be found electronically and a decision made automatically to make or buy. That decision will be merged with resource and manufacturing planning data to approve the request and generate an electronic order. Material and services will be sent to the appropriate location, preceded by an advance shipping notice. Receipt and delivery information will be electronically transmitted to the central processing location, with financial information being generated to match the transactions. Suppliers will be paid electronically, and all necessary postdelivery reporting will be provided. All of this will be conducted over an Internet-type link that uses joint data repositories to make all transactions visible to the constituents. Order status

EXHIBIT 9.5
An E-Commerce-Enabled Purchasing Process

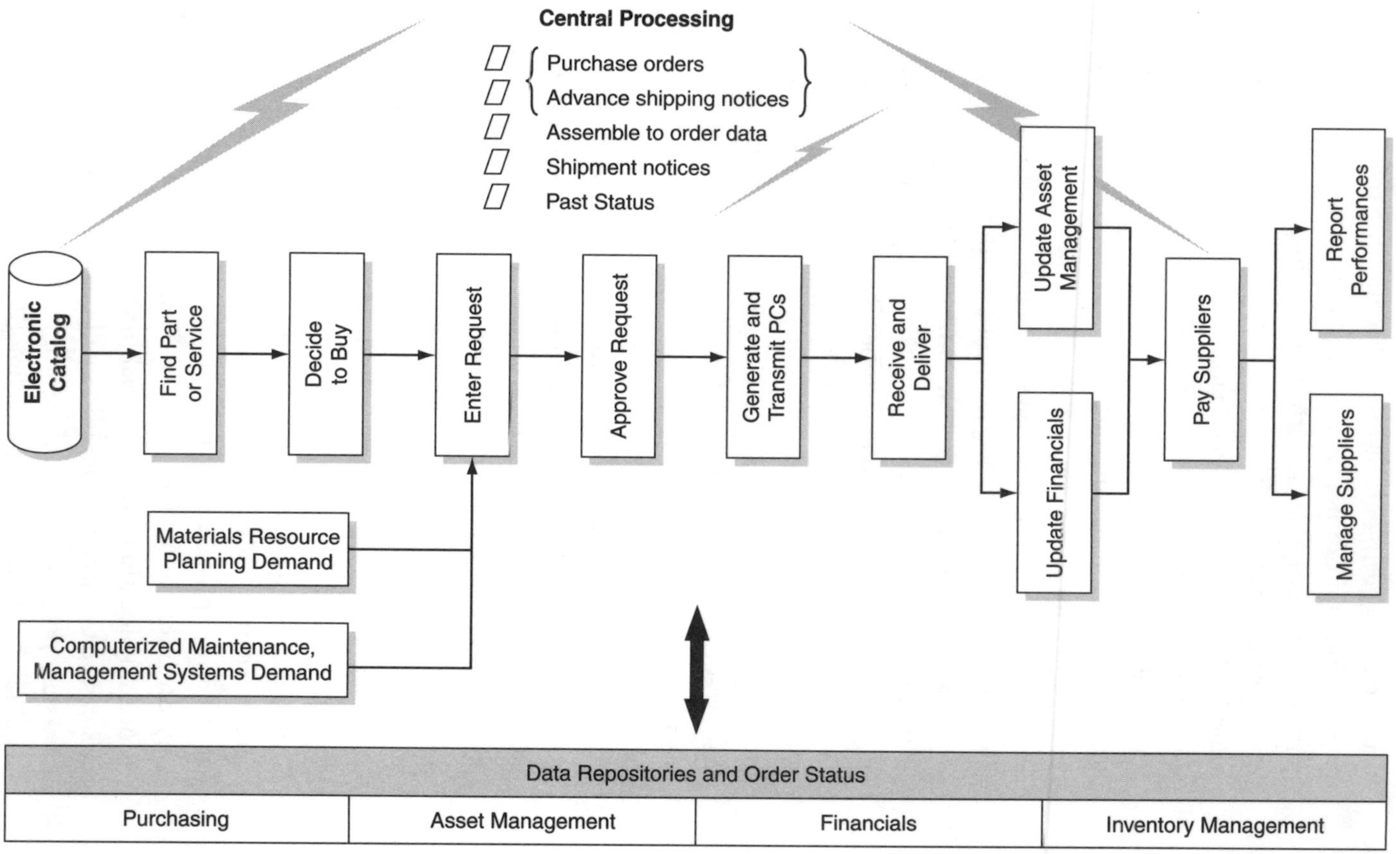

Central Processing

{ Purchase orders
{ Advance shipping notices
Assemble to order data
Shipment notices
Past Status

Electronic Catalog → Find Part or Service → Decide to Buy → Enter Request → Approve Request → Generate and Transmit PCs → Receive and Deliver → Update Asset Management / Update Financials → Pay Suppliers → Report Performances / Manage Suppliers

Materials Resource Planning Demand → Enter Request

Computerized Maintenance, Management Systems Demand → Enter Request

Data Repositories and Order Status			
Purchasing	Asset Management	Financials	Inventory Management

is checked and inventory managed over the Internet, and financial communication is on-line and in real time.

▶ Providing the Necessary Focus

The *focus* for the constellation is on consumers of choice and the network of supply. To support the effort at this level, traditional channel structures must be challenged, as they may not have kept pace with the changing demand structure. The typical problems of slow product introductions, scarcity and allocation problems, inventory obsolescence, and unpredictable service levels can be solved when the network members focus on the simplest and most effective way to bring goods and services to specific consumers. Out-of-the-box thinking is crucial in this area to combat the tendency to regard existing systems as the best possible.

> *To support the effort at this level, traditional channel structures must be challenged, as they may not have kept pace with the changing demand structure.*

When the gains are documented, value chain members will be encouraged to pursue cooperation even more enthusiastically. The steering committee must play a central role in this effort. Because there is often a temptation to drift back to point solutions (at a particular hand-off in the supply chain) created by one particular member of the network, the committee must continually emphasize solutions across the total value chain alliance.

The leadership teams must insist on reviewing the outputs of the various action teams that come into existence, making certain that benefit for the alliance is at the heart of suggested changes. This challenge is particularly important as the interactive systems are designed and will guide the cooperative efforts. Advanced technology and communication systems have increasingly enhanced efficiency throughout manufacturing, service, and supply chain activities. Opportunities for unprecedented improvements have raised the bar for adding value throughout a supply chain. Smooth integration of activities among the supply chain constituents is crucial for reaping the full benefits of these dramatic changes at Level IV. Success requires more than mere advocacy of integration; it depends on actual documentation of integration results.

▶ The Utmost Importance of Technology

The ubiquitous availability of networked information causes fundamental changes in a typical business environment, making it imperative for solutions to be implemented across the entire alliance of business partners for best results. Cross-discipline and cross-organizational teams can succeed in redesigning interactive business processes enabled by Web-based technology. Unless they are selling a unique product or service, businesses that fail to transform will be forced to catch up to the leaders because of competitive pressures or else lose market share.

Exhibit 9.6 is a projection by Computer Sciences Corporation of the market size of Internet commerce, expected to grow to almost $350 billion by 2002. Still in its infancy, the growth projections are astounding for myriad industries. Financial services offered over the Web represented $1.2 billion in 1997 sales and are expected to grow to $5 billion by 2001. Books and music rang up $156 million in 1997, with a 2001 projection of $1.1 billion. The travel industry is expected to account for 35 percent of on-line sales by 2002, up from 11 percent in 1998, as this industry forges ahead with its Internet-based consumers. Business-to-business sales in general are predicted to rise from $8 billion in 1997 to $183 billion by 2001. (All of the specific industry projections are courtesy of Forrester Research, Inc.) The sheer mass and size of this new market makes it essential for a supply network to work out the details of how to access this communication medium and exploit it for new revenues.

The *tools* of these high-technology interfaces will be intranet, Internet, and extranet systems. For the purposes of this discussion, the following definitions will be used:

> *Intranet:* A private and relatively expensive electronic network whereby a nucleus organization and its internal constituents are given access to privileged information permitting them to

EXHIBIT 9.6
Internet Commerce: About to Explode

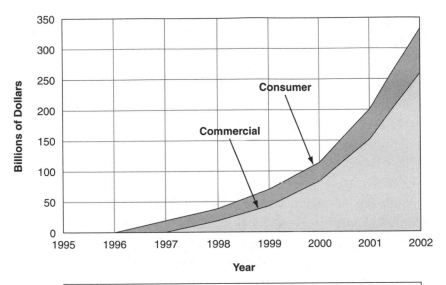

According to one estimate, Web-based commerce will grow from
$5 billion in December 1996 to more than $200 billion in December 2001

Source: International Data Service.

add value to supply chain processing. Intranets are secure and
allow individual employees to share information using the
same protocols and standards as the Internet. This network can
be extended to selected suppliers and distributors for the purpose of speeding product development and concept-to-market
activities, as well as improving the distribution efficiency. The
problem is that the investments in costly private networks and
customized software make the intranet impractical for low-
volume transactions.

Internet: The worldwide public electronic network, a relatively inexpensive forum where value chain constellation information
can be presented, appropriate for improving the system of supply and for transferring important information on product,
costs, availability, specifications, and ordering possibilities. Use
of the Internet is best focused on specific consumer groups that

will find the network advantages of importance in their buying decisions.

Extranet: A private network designed to use the Internet for data
transfer, allowing certain people to share data from an internal
and external environment. Designed collaboratively, it becomes
a system carrying privileged information and linking organizations together to address specific market opportunities. The
network should include suppliers, distributors, and key customers by which the products and services will be taken to the
consumers of choice.

The excursion into this technology begins on an internal basis and
rapidly expands to an external basis before solidifying for a specific
constellation. Intranets are the preliminary developments. Firms have
discovered great value in linking internal parties to a simple and inexpensive means of sharing data to shorten cycles, increase probabilities
of success, and reduce costs. Hewlett-Packard has a world-class
intranet, linking product developers around the world so that product development can continue on a twenty-four-hour-a-day basis. Key
suppliers are linked into this system, so there is no delay in getting
critical parts into the design of a new printer or multipurpose office
machine. Work on a new device might be started in the United States
in the morning and be continued on the other side of the world (per-
haps in India) while the Americans get some sleep. Intranets are
becoming the medium of choice and are already very popular as a way
to manage knowledge inside a firm. These systems speed the transfer
of accurate, on-line data across internal computers. Documented supply chain savings include elimination of paper, reduced time to market, reduced fixed costs, fast on-line transactions, reduced costs of
shared services, reduced complexity of transactions, "disintermediation" (elimination of a process and transfer to a more able source),
new marketing techniques, and collaborative solution creation.

The important factor is to make certain that the new opportunities are linked firmly to the business plans. When value chain constellations catch up and pass competing networks in digital space, it
will be the solid connection between the use of real-time or accurate
on-line information, clearly linked to network objectives, that will
make the advantage significant. When new channels and markets are

set up and exploited, the ones with a focused consumer base will make the most progress.

Exhibit 9.7 shows the four steps in a logical development pattern for an interactive communication system. Phase 1 begins with assessing the readiness of the business network that will take advantage of this powerful tool. With a joint vision and strategy, the network moves to Phase 2, where the technology architecture is defined and an organizational model is established. In Phase 3, the organizations begin on-line operations, most often with a pilot test to prove the validity of the systems design. In Phase 4, the strategy is checked against results, and necessary fine-tuning is performed. Throughout the cycle, a project management team with cross-organizational membership monitors the cycle for flaws and necessary adjustment.

EXHIBIT 9.7
Developing a Digital Life Cycle

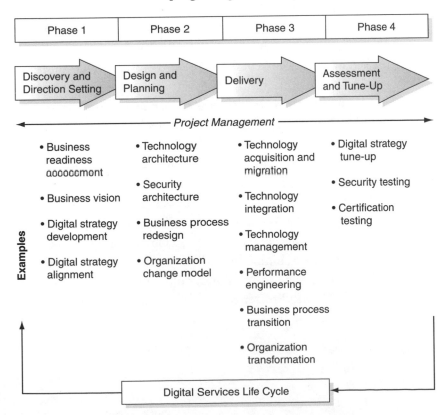

Chapter 10

Using Technology to Hold an Advantage

As business offerings, use of technology, and consumer satisfaction converge into a defining strategy for achieving market advantage, the common ingredient will be information technology used to outperform a competing network. Just as Wal-Mart overcame Sears through superior logistical systems, so can many other firms use information technology (infotech) to overtake their competitors. The ingredients are cheap and available worldwide. The secret is using infotech superiority to gain and protect the advantage. The leaders are already hard at work. Federal Express maintains an infotech system that is considered by many analysts to be a year ahead of its competitors, as it allows customers to track their own shipments on-line in real time. Wal-Mart has been setting the pace in retailing for years, and its network with Procter & Gamble is still considered the defining model.

▶ A Network Focus

Developing the digital strategy must involve network participation to answer several key questions:

- ▶ What new business opportunities and capabilities are being offered by the World Wide Web, the Internet, and digital commerce? What can we do better with the Net?
- ▶ What operational, strategic, and policy issues should be addressed? How do we protect confidential information? How do we share the costs of development?
- ▶ What are the key cultural differences between the current markets and the emerging "digital market"? Which consumers of choice can be reached through the Web?
- ▶ What impact will the growth of the Internet have on the information technology used today by the constituents of the value chain constellation? Are parts of existing systems already obsolete?

A constellation attempts to use information technology as the new tool of success in an open market that is dominated by peer-to-peer relationships, and answers to these questions help build the foundation for joint exploitation of new markets. As answers are developed to guide the construction, another series of queries comes up, oriented heavily around market participants:

- ▶ Who are my specific targeted consumers, and how do they use the Internet? What demographic information is available to guide development?
- ▶ How do I use the Net to maintain and enhance the image of our value chain constellation?
- ▶ How can we expand our reach to new markets and customers? How global should our reach become?

▶ How are competing networks using these new capabilities? What current information can we access?

▶ How can we use the Internet to gather intelligence on competitors legally?

▶ In what ways will advertising and branding strategies be affected by the Internet culture?

These questions raise further questions about what to introduce over the Web and how initially to use the Internet. Products appealing to the technologically agile consumer are always at the top of the list. This means that not all products will sell successfully over the Web. Demographic information about Internet users can be helpful. Of particular interest to Web buyers seem to be computer-related items and products that are simple and clear—reservations, flowers, travel and event tickets, and so forth. Hard-to-find specialty items and collectibles about which people have a passion also do well.

It is important to consider not just what consumers want but also how to use the Internet as a precursor to developing an extranet that can enhance competitive advantage. Companies can modify the portfolio of offerings on the Web as they proceed from pilots to actual, real-time situations. The data used over the extranet can help the constituents apply their limited resources more effectively. Such a situation arises when the parties to the network realize that working through a linked information system establishes a framework for allocating resources and setting up Web priorities. The value chain partners recognize that they are creating not some large monolith but multiple information components integrated with a core vision. The real focus should be on delivery of added business value rather than technology. Technology functions as the enabler and the communication conduit. Wise firms use technology not for the sake of being in front of a curve but for addressing the business-to-business technical, process, and people issues of importance to a value chain constellation.

> *Companies can modify the portfolio of offerings on the Web as they proceed from pilots to actual, real-time situations.*

▶ Web Consumer Power

The rising influence of infotech is placing increasing power in the hands of customers and consumers. Armed with accurate, complete, and up-to-date information, buyers are able to check prices and specifications offered around the globe, instantly and continually. In business-to-customer selling, these advances are evidenced by dramatic changes in what is now a very active electronic commerce system of interaction. Consumers are using the Internet to buy cars, computers, books, magazines, insurance, stocks and bonds, airline reservations, and much more. In business-to-business selling, industrial buyers are accessing electronic catalogs to order subassemblies and components and to secure small parts and services. Firms such as W. W. Grainger are selling maintenance, repair, and operating (MRO) supplies over the World Wide Web.

Many companies are marching forward on the Web, displaying a wide range of components, materials, parts, and all manner of products that can be used by manufacturers. Buyers are finding new ways to work with engineers to select parts, components, and assemblies from suppliers that meet specifications and quality standards, all over electronic connections. Electronic supplier catalogs are getting better at displaying features and setting prices. E-commerce is the new wave of doing business—a way to sell innovation and service to any consumer anywhere in the world. E-commerce will displace catalog buying, with a change in emphasis from raw material and finished goods inventory to the total spent by the network.

The purpose of infotech is to create network solutions to the interrelated process problems that constitute the interenterprise network. The important caveat is that the IT plans must fit with the intentions of the overall business strategies. As infotech becomes an increasingly indispensable component of business success, leaders need to synchronize their plans with strategies directing the overall network of firms constituting the value chain constellation. In the years to come, technology will play the central role, making it possible for allied companies to define differentiating strategies for their value chain constellations.

The technology destined to play the major role is the Internet. For 77 percent of the respondents to CSC's 1997 Critical Issues of Information Systems Management study, the Internet is one of the most important tools they must adopt in order to remain competitive. Two other network-related technologies—electronic commerce and groupware—also rated highly on the respondents' list of critical emerging technologies. As Philip Manchester (1997, p. 47) reported in the *Financial Post,* "It seems that, when the Internet comes into the supply chain, it also changes the structure of the market. Companies in some markets, therefore, can no longer view the Internet only as an option: they must view it as an essential communications channel to their customers and their suppliers."

Exhibit 10.1 shows schematically how this essential Internet channel will interface with supply chain processes. External business drivers dealing with the designated markets to be entered, penetrated, or

EXHIBIT 10.1
Internet: The First Medium to Create and Fulfill Demand

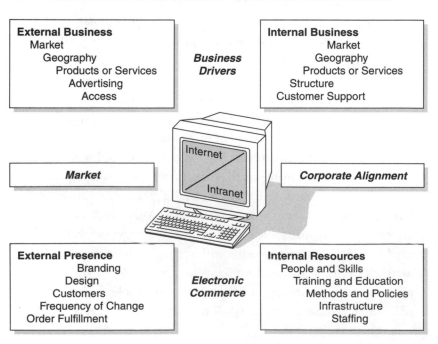

nurtured—and in what geographical locations—are combining with the products and services offered and with choices of advertising and promotions. Decisions about who should have access also affect the business, and linkage across the value chain constellation completes the view. Internal business drivers that deal with how well a company can reach the market in geographical sites with the desired products and services is matched with the previous input to determine if the current structure will suffice and what additional customer support is necessary. This portion of the analysis invariably reveals a need for partnering with selected network allies.

Using the intranet first, the constituents access the mutual pool of resources. The objective is to determine where there are sufficient or insufficient resources in terms of people, skills, education, and training. In short, the network infrastructure is linked so that the leaders can quickly determine where support is needed, particularly in terms of the methods and policies that will guide the sharing of resources and rewards.

> *In short, the network infrastructure is linked so that the leaders can quickly determine where support is needed, particularly in terms of the methods and policies that will guide the sharing of resources and rewards.*

Moving to the Internet and the advantages of electronic commerce, the network begins to assess its external presence and looks for ways to increase penetration through branding, new design, customer-specific initiatives, frequency of change, new product introduction, and world-class order fulfillment.

While the goal is to move externally as fast as possible at Level IV, some learning must precede the development of a complete value chain constellation. Exhibit 10.2 shows the migration that typically occurs on the way to advanced stages of Internet sharing. In the early steps of cooperation and interaction, the Web is used to communicate. This is a period of testing and development. As network partners learn to use their new tool and develop the advanced levels of trust necessary for proceeding, they make the transition to selling products and services in the transaction stage. With success will come the partnering stage, in which the network delivers products and services digitally, across a virtual network of supply.

EXHIBIT 10.2
Digital Business Value Migration

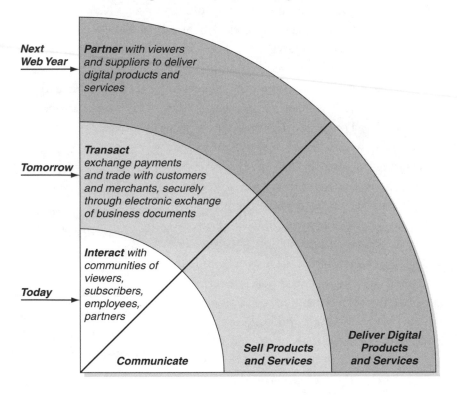

This leads to the era of individual interactive marketing (IIM), the latest extension of mass customization, as shown in Exhibit 10.3.

In this era, consumers will be able to meet their needs through a simplified shopping format, with an unprecedented variety of choice. The firm that avoids this wave of change will risk being left out of the loop by one of the largest segments of future consumers. Today there are 50 million Internet users, and the number is growing exponentially. Demographics of this user class are very attractive, including average income of $63,000, with 13 percent having annual income in excess of $100,000. The result of participation will be more sales, higher margins, and lower costs. The technology that is already available to integrate Web front-end interactions with back-office systems include packaged Web modules, "middleware" and

EXHIBIT 10.3
Individual Interactive Marketing

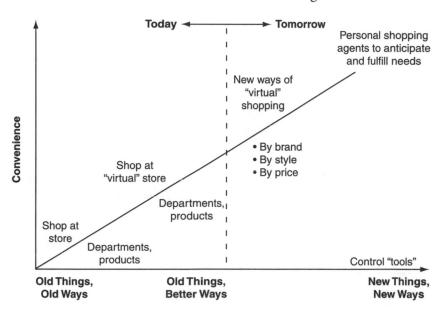

tools to build customized transaction systems, Web-based EDI, Web-based electronic marketplaces, and a plethora of start-up electronic catalogs.

What is becoming clear is the emergence of what can be called digital business value chains, described schematically in Exhibit 10.4.

Already pioneered by Charles Schwab in brokering, Michael Dell in computer configuration, Visa in credit services, and Nike in shoes and athletic apparel, this type of network connection allows the consumer to go directly to the system of choice to design, configure, and arrange for shipment of the final product of choice. This ability is the result of an extranet linking partners in supply to the necessary information on-line, in real time. An intranet is used to link the technologies, business processes, and the organizational constituencies into a network that can display its offerings over the Internet, bringing special value to the consumers who prefer this medium. Exhibit 10.5 illustrates simply how such a network can be constructed.

Suppliers of necessary components (in the case of Dell Computers, drives, memory, keyboards, and other items) are linked electronically

EXHIBIT 10.4
Digital Business Value Chain

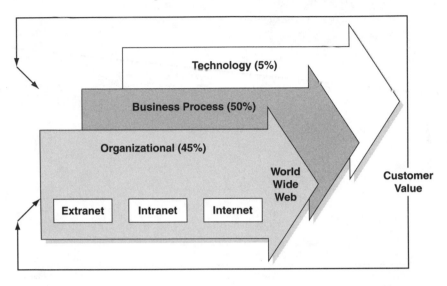

with assembly and integration sites (many of which may not be owned by the manufacturer or service provider). Transport providers and information managers are also linked into the network. When customers enter orders, the system reacts by creating the final product or service and sending it, via the market-facing entity, directly to the customer via the appropriate medium. This type of network offers the best answer in terms of flexibility and simplicity. It is a means of obtaining increased value at a decreased cost with several options.

▶ Interenterprise Reliance

With the necessary technological tools in place, the *action area* for the constellation becomes the full enterprise of choice. This area of concentration may have always been intended, but only in the advanced stages of supply chain performance do actions coalesce to permit network solutions to be leveraged for the mutual advantage of the constituents.

EXHIBIT 10.5
Value Networks to Serve Customers

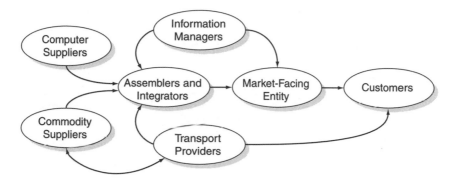

A major new feature will be the introduction of collaborative planning across the network. Using features that will create a "glass pipeline" (to be described shortly), the members begin working closely to develop a means of planning together so that the availability of materials and supplies is linked with manufacturing and delivery schedules in such a way that any constituent can call up the data and know, with high reliability, what is in the pipeline. Exhibit 10.6 shows a general map of needed developments.

Pioneered by Sun Microsystems, this process improvement is meant for a Level IV effort, when the parties to the value chain constellation are ready to link themselves into a system that makes planning easier, faster, and more accurate, with far less inventory, buffer, and safety stocks.

Under most current systems, the planning is disjointed because it is performed independently by the various links in the supply chain. Suppliers plan their shipments of needed raw materials on the basis of forecasts of spurious value. Extra stocks are stored at supplying locations to ensure that no machine shuts down due to lack of available supplies. The manufacturer, working from some sort of rolling forecast with the retail customers, will be designing responses, planning current manufacturing and assembly schedules, and arranging the logistical means of getting the finished goods to a distributor or a direct customer. This process requires very accurate data and

EXHIBIT 10.6
Achieving Collaborative Planning

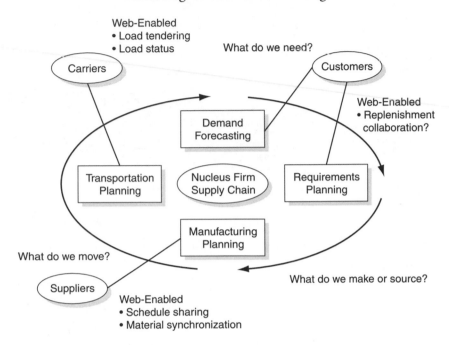

analysis before dispatching orders to the factory floor—in fact, it requires a level of accuracy that is almost impossible to achieve.

This is a tired system in dire need of fixing. Using collaborative planning, the suppliers, distributors, and key customers can achieve several major improvements:

- Faster reaction to market demands with swifter deliveries of the right products and services
- Reduced cycle times from initial supply to final delivery and from new concept to commercialization
- Increased inventory turns across the network while eliminating phantom stocks and obsolescence
- Instant view of customer requirements and the system of response and replenishment
- Maximum use of assets and new capital investment

The new system will require the nucleus company to begin the linkage, by connecting with suppliers via the Internet with a user-friendly system (in Sun's case, that means Java). The connection is from the host firm's central master planning in conjunction with on-line access to the customer's enterprise resource planning (ERP) system, to the key suppliers' shop floor information, and to any necessary interface with distribution planning. All of this is performed via an interconnected, tightly fused extranet. This type of system maximizes responsiveness, eliminating the normal delays involved in waiting for answers to telephone calls, faxes, and emergency expediting requests, which in this system are on-line in real time. Supporting information is visible, and capacities and schedules are preprogrammed for proper reaction. Cooperation that is now based on clean data and supported by intelligent processes shortens response times from weeks to minutes. Choices are clearly displayed on the interactive screens, allowing "what if?" scenarios to be conducted and brought to a logical conclusion.

The goal is to move the interconnected organizations from an intraenterprise view of the world to a global supply chain–centric environment (the interenterprise approach). By deploying together over the Internet, with Java-based or equivalent-enabled tools such as advanced planning, value sourcing, order fulfillment, and the newly linked ERP systems, firms will extend their reach beyond the internal walls of their own manufacturing expertise. They will begin reaping the rewards of an integrated network solution and will establish stronger ties with the selected consumer group. By taking advantage of current technology that is focused on supply chain improvement, the involved companies will increase their ability to respond to customer and market demands while reducing the cost of that response. They will build the "glass pipeline" of visible material and service flow desired by today's customers and consumers.

Guidance in this new world of collaboration will derive from linked demand and supply information that unites the constituents in providing the best solutions that capitalize on their combined synergy and symbiosis. The resulting network focuses totally on serving the targeted consumers while taking full advantage of each partner's strength. The final consumer senses the product or service as customized for his or her own special benefit. With much cleaner data based on actual consumption and demand, the supply network will place the right goods and services at a point of consumption that is not only easy to access but also conveys an impression of extraordinary value to the purchaser.

The risk of marketing or production failure is minimized because decisions involving replenishment and new product introduction will be guided by true patterns of consumer buying. Whether the final sale is made at a giant warehouse location in a major city or at a tiny crossroads convenience store in a remote area of Montana, consumption information is visible and allows highly efficient resupply.

> *The risk of marketing or production failure is minimized because decisions involving replenishment and new product introduction will be guided by true patterns of consumer buying.*

Performance metrics will become network-focused as activity-based costing gains importance. Summary statements track benefits from supply to consumption. New elements of cooperation, such as supply chain compression, collaborative planning, and collaborative design, are measured to determine how much positive impact each constituent has received. These statements will initially be used to identify the gap between current performance and what could be attained through an advanced network approach but will eventually measure progress in eliminating this gap and in satisfying customers.

▶ Global Enterprise in Perspective

Leading change in an industry is a challenge, but that is what several insightful firms are doing in their quest to become unchallenged front-runners. As they redefine their penetration of a market, they create a conceptual change that affects the entire industry. One of the most dynamic of those changes comes with the simplification of traditional relationships with consumers, customers, distributors, manufacturers, and suppliers. This redesign and simplification have been occurring for some time and have resulted in some firms' achieving dominance in their industries. An additional advantage is these leaders' ability to establish a *transparent* environment in which decisions are easy because the right choices are readily understood and obvious. It is a working environment framed in honesty and trust, free of arrogance and deceit—this is what is becoming known as the *glass pipeline* of supply.

Most Level I and II supply chains are opaque, not transparent. Information transfer is clouded by an absence of reliable and necessary data. Some networks have progressed to the point where reliable information on inventory availability is generated, allowing the value chain constellation to create a real available-to-promise condition. Transparency in a supply chain begins when the interconnected members are ready to put the results of their network on display in a glass pipeline, showing the customer and consumer a virtual inventory—where the goods and services are, in what quantities, at what prices, and when deliveries can reliably be made.

The complications that occur across a typical chain of supply offer too many opportunities for mistakes and failures, creating distrust and confusion. That explains a great deal of consumer dissatisfaction and deteriorating loyalty to branded products being sold globally. Yet great opportunities for improvement exist for the evolving value chain constellations. Firms that want to establish a Level IV network in which decision making is easy for the consumer must at least pilot a product line or service that can be shown through a glass pipeline. This requires a network linkage containing all information necessary to show the flow of materials and construction in order for the consumer to follow it, much like watching a house being built.

To illustrate, consider a consumer product heading to market. We'll begin at the consumer level, where a specific person identifies the need to purchase a particular product. Retailers invest large amounts of marketing dollars in anticipation of this action. They do all they can to understand consumer shopping habits and to satisfy such needs at the lowest possible prices. They will attempt to have the right amount of the right products on display or readily available so that sales can be booked at the time of the impulse to buy. On occasion, they will promote certain products in an effort to pull demand forward. All of this is done on an invisible basis to the consumer until the advertisement for the product is received, a coupon is clipped, or the consumer comes into the store and sees the product of choice. That is today's model.

Consider the new model, in which the consumer has access to an on-line electronic catalog that displays all available offerings and can make special reference to the desired item. On the viewing screen, this consumer can also see the flow of materials to the point of purchase and can know exactly how long replacement products will take, in the event that the item is not currently available. Details on usage and specifications are included, as well as current pricing. Now the opaque has become transparent.

Pass now to the retailer, who has access to the same glass pipeline of information. With accurate demand information, the retailer now interfaces at the distributor level, where a decision can be made regarding how much stock to transfer to the store (or directly to the consumer). If the retailer has been clever enough to get the consumer to transfer information about future purchases, this decision is facilitated for tomorrow's needs. Armed with actual consumption data that is updated every hour, the retailer no longer invests in unnecessary safety stocks and saves valuable floor and shelf space for the most active items for the consumers who still insist on coming to the store for their purchases.

More important, the retailer now has a direct link to the consumer. Recent studies confirm that store loyalty is slipping. With so many choices, the average shopper splits time between alternative locations. With a direct electronic linkage, the retailer has an opportunity to tune into specific needs and direct promotions on a specific basis. It no longer becomes a case of always having the lowest price or the largest assortment but rather entails having the currently demanded items readily available (even by direct delivery), backed by simple and adequate service. With a renewed sense of loyalty comes the opportunity for more profitable pricing.

While all of this activity is occurring over the Web, the distributor can now decide what products to stock and when and where to make shipments. The number of stock-keeping units is reduced because speculation on the variety of items necessary to meet demand has been replaced by direct knowledge of what is being consumed. Consumers are drowning in a sea of nonessential variety today. A recent trip through a local supermarket revealed over 150 SKUs for dog food! This is the sort of proliferation of stock items that raises cost for distributors and retailers without adding real consumer pull-through or providing true consumer advantage. Thanks to a direct link to the preferred consumer, information on items that are truly in demand will be accurate and current.

With this on-line information regarding consumer preference and consumption, the distributor moves to an active role in category management and takes responsibility for stocking the store shelves with pull-through items. This is not a new practice, but it is one that can be greatly facilitated by the glass pipeline, taking the mystery out of what the retailer should put on display. If a product is in stock on the shelf, there is a chance it has been there too long. Armed with the current information and the demand input from the consumer, the distributor can decide if it is still "fresh" or needs to be replaced. Developing improved "planograms," based on real-time consumption data, can simplify the process of replenishment in a substantial way. By simplifying the entire decision process, each constituent can refocus energy on adding value to the supply network.

> *The manufacturer can now use resources that were previously allocated to expediting because of the poor information coming through the opaque system of yesterday to create value-added marketing and product development.*

The manufacturer can now use resources that were previously allocated to expediting because of the poor information coming through the opaque system of yesterday to create value-added marketing and product development. Retailers can invest in analyzing consumer shopping needs and can interface with key consumer groups to anticipate changing buying habits. With greater transparency, the distributors can more efficiently determine what products best meet retailers' objectives while sustaining high consumer satisfaction ratings (which are now being quickly gathered over the response portion of the glass pipeline). Distributors' category managers are working on-line with the manufacturers and retailers, ensuring that the right goods are flowing through at optimal speeds and costs.

All of these activities result in better collaboration across the value chain constellation with a great increase in customer satisfaction. The relationships become far less confrontational and adversarial as they move toward a more rational and data-based arrangement. As Robert Elliot, a manager at Peat Marwick, told *Fortune* magazine: "If the supply chain is transparent, with all the information visible, you can create the most value with the least resources" (Kupfner, 1998, p. 95).

If you think the on-line glass pipeline is a mere vision for the distant future, consider that on-line buying is expected to reach $4.8 billion in 1998 (Green and De George, 1998, p. 90), with electronic commerce bringing a vast new marketplace into being. The Internet is where the retailers of tomorrow will have to be. With its famed build-to-order model, Dell Computer is reportedly ringing up $3 million per day through its Web connections. When a consumer clicks "yes" on Dell's Web site, the personal computer manufacturer relays on-line orders directly to assemblers. That seamless link of information between user and value chain constellation creates the product and delivers a custom-designed PC to the consumer.

Hotel, car, and airline reservations are already well on their way to an established presence in the new medium. Flowers have been sold on-line for some time. Businesses will exchange an estimated $17 billion in goods and services this year over the Internet, according to Forrester Research, Inc. The forecast for e-commerce by the year 2002 is $349 billion. Boeing has booked $100 million in spare parts, ordered from airlines in the past year through a Web site that took just seven months to build (Hof, McWilliams, and Saveri, 1998).

As the number of people dialing into the Web accelerates, many brand-name companies are opening up new shops. On January 16, 1998, Office Depot launched its on-line store, complete with Dilbert, the wisecracking cartoon character, as its on-line sales representative, helping "cybershoppers" find what they're looking for and walking with them through their first on-line purchase (Green, De George, and Barrett, 1998). Office Depot has decided that Dilbert is one means of making the interactive experience more palatable to first-time users. Following close behind are such names as Bloomingdale's,

The Gap, Sears, and Clinique. Books are now selling like gangbusters through Amazon.com, with Barnes & Noble and Borders right behind. An army of marketers is preparing its offerings for introduction to this medium. The most successful ones will be supported with the kind of virtual linkage we have described. The lesson is clear: move to the Internet with a glass pipeline that makes the flow of products and services transparent and simplifies the process of manufacturing, marketing, selling, and delivering.

▶ A Global Model

The *model* of choice, for constellations moving into Level IV, will be one that brings attention to the global market. Nothing less will suffice. For wholly domestic supply chains, a modified version might be used for a point solution, but it will miss the opportunities that exist for firms of any size to capitalize on global sourcing. Information technology has so shrunk the business arena that the only wise approach to optimizing a supply chain is the global one.

The 3M Company recently performed an extensive evaluation of supply chains for all of its divisions, and its experience helps illustrate the point (Arntzen, Mulgrew, and Sjolander, 1998). In the middle of a three-year effort, termed the Supply Chain Excellence (SCE) initiative, this St. Paul, Minnesota–based organization is attempting to "be the most innovative enterprise in the world" and the "preferred supplier in the markets we serve." The participants advise that "redesigning a global supply chain is not an endeavor to be taken lightly" and that "managing a supply chain in a large, multinational company is much easier said than done." Indeed, it is an endeavor to be undertaken only when a company has progressed to Level III or IV. A typical but simplified international supply chain model, taken from the consumer product division of 3M, is depicted in Exhibit 10.7.

In this model, orders from customers around the globe trigger a demand pattern that is quickly translated into a flow of raw materials (most likely including global sources) to a manufacturing bill of materials (that could include subassemblies or outsourced components) to

EXHIBIT 10.7
A Global Product Supply Network

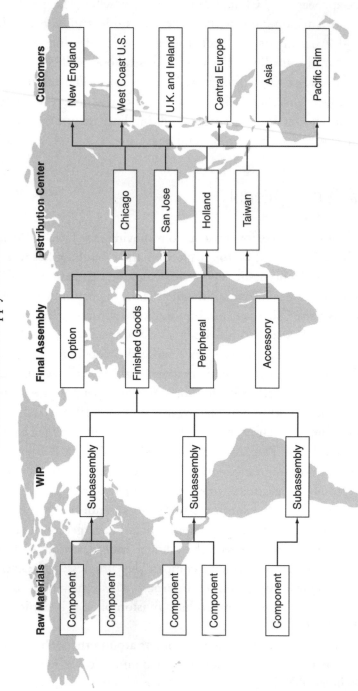

Source: Arntzen, Mulgrew, and Sjolander, 1998, p. 18. Reprinted with permission of Cahners Business Information.

an assembly operation where the final products are configured or assembled. The finished goods then flow through global distribution centers for delivery to the final consumer. As the architects of the 3M model point out (Arntzen et al., 1998, p. 18), in contrast to traditional distribution network analysis (the internal view), a global supply chain design considers

- The whole supply chain (raw materials, vendors, plants, warehouses, merge points, and customers)
- Time (vendor lead times, production cycle times and transit times) as well as costs
- International trade factors (duty, duty drawback, international taxes, local content, offset trade, transfer prices, currency exchange)
- Multiple modes of transportation (ocean, air, road, rail, and so on)

These are factors that must be taken into consideration as a multi-organizational team begins to diagram a very complex set of supply and delivery operations. When the team goes forward with the simplification and compression process, opportunities will appear for reducing the size and complexity of the diagram. Most efforts in this area result in dramatic improvements while giving due consideration to all of the factors listed. As the international factors are considered, it becomes apparent just how difficult it is for a single firm to cope with all of the interrelated dynamics. The assistance of qualified allies will not only facilitate this process but will also introduce innovative ideas and concepts that would otherwise be missed in the improvement process.

> *As the international factors are considered, it becomes apparent just how difficult it is for a single firm to cope with all of the interrelated dynamics.*

An alternative pursued by Level II firms has been to segment the chain of supply and to use experts in each sector of the model. However, the integration process falters when one member of the network lacks the required capabilities; this weak link typically weakens the entire chain. Purchasing, for example, might have found a very reliable, low-cost source for an important subassembly, but a more efficient manufacturing process could result by using an alternative (almost as good) source. A better approach is to develop the entire supply network with interacting teams, where efforts are closely coordinated through constant communication and periodic reviews. Fortunately, software is available that will help in the process.

For 3M, the effort in the consumer products area was considered very successful and is expected to reduce supply chain costs by 17 percent by the year 2001. Based on these results, 3M has established a new manufacturing strategy for this division and set in place a cross-functional advanced effort with a source of supply (SOS) guidance team. In the future, this team will update and rerun the model as changes are encountered and will expand the effort to other applications within 3M. The company may benefit by expanding the amount of external participation in the process as nondomestic sources of help could offer the out-of-the-box thinking necessary to achieve true Level IV performance.

▶ Few Single Organizations in Level IV

Alliances will be an imperative in Level IV. Joint ventures are often the vehicle by which mutual resources are applied. As has been emphasized, no single firm can move effectively into a Level IV position by itself. It takes the cooperation and active participation of a chain of constituents, working in concert with a focus on a specific market and consumer group. These potential alliances may be formed in pre–Level IV stages, but they must be firmly established in this final level. Application of mutual resources and capital investments are central actions in Level IV, actions that can be accomplished effectively only when the alliances have gone beyond the informal stage to a near-contract state.

Training remains a future opportunity, as yet undefined. A great potential awaits the organizations prepared to capitalize on this new area of concentration. As the alliances solidify, there will be a need to train the cross-organizational participants in how to function in a constellation environment. This training will be collaborative and will add a new dimension to teaming, with representation from many (often conflicting) cultures.

In Chapter 11, we will take a futuristic look at how cooperation and integration can be brought to bear on business activities. For now, we conclude that Level IV is a beacon of what can happen but requires new levels of trust and cooperation not currently available with some of the most advanced supply networks. Alliances and training are yet to be defined for these constellations, but they must move beyond the formative stages to full acceptance if they are to realize the complete benefits of collaboration.

Chapter 11

A Vision of the Future: Turbocharging the Supply Chain

The four levels of progression in the supply chain evolution have been described. A firm must now choose how it wishes to advance along the continuum. The firm must recognize that it cannot make this journey alone. Companies that want to be industry leaders realize they must reinvent the total network in which they are merely one player. To achieve such leadership, a firm must cooperate in creating the value chain constellation that will dominate an industry. This network consists of a linked set of agile companies that not only react to market challenges but in fact dynamically anticipate and exploit new opportunities that can sustain profitable revenue growth and exceptional shareholder value well into the next decade.

Considering the importance of targeting markets and consumers, a company must also choose its value chain partners very carefully because they are the key to future profits and competitive advantage. In short, alliances must be built with organizations that are qualified to assist in the process. Leading-edge companies that recognize this fact are already working with compatible partners, leveraging the core competencies of each ally into a network of unparalleled efficiency. These firms' joint objective is to optimize the total effort and respond to customers and consumers faster, more efficiently, and more accurately than ever before, supported by a seamless supply chain. Making the transition from an internal to an external focus with the help of these allies has proved to be the hardest part of the journey, primarily because of instinctive fears and a general lack of trust. However, visionary firms desiring the same end point, willing to build trust and security into the value chain constellation, can overcome these fears.

With the road map laid out and the destination defined, value chain partners can pursue a jointly determined set of process improvement initiatives based on what works for other networks or on new and innovative designs created by the members of the value chain constellation. As companies reach Level IV, they see a clear vision of future success. They realize exciting opportunities for supply chain efficiencies, profits, and competitive strength that could never be achieved by a single firm working in isolation, no matter how "perfect" its internal improvements may be.

Those who fear the journey can take comfort from the new information technology, which makes the value chain constellation not only possible but in fact necessary. Firms making this transition to Level IV will continue to rely on well-known, traditional linear business models, but they must go beyond the models by including and cooperating with all partners in the network, who function much like a traditional peer group, defining and developing the transition initiatives together. The central driving force behind the transition will be a nucleus company, using a nontraditional circular or mushroom-shaped model and controlling the value of the major brands being taken to market. Both nontraditional business models will be considered in this chapter.

To help explain this evolution to Level IV, let us open our minds through a reverie, a dream of what can be achieved in this most advanced stage of supply chain management. Let us consider the kind of benefits that can accrue for the leading value chain constellation in a particular industry. Let us view the meaning of being first to the most advanced stage, a position in which "network" signifies profitable revenue growth, increased shareholder value, and competitive advantage.

▶ The Value of Optimizing a Value Chain Constellation

Level IV offers a means of achieving unprecedented levels of profitability and efficiency. Suppose that these revenues are 10 to 20 percent above the business plan. Imagine that profits can be increased by 30 to 50 percent, cycle times reduced by 20 to 50 percent, and inventory as a percentage of revenue cut in half. Add to the dream the fact that shareholder value rises because of a doubling in earnings per share, and customer satisfaction reaches new highs.

These results can be achieved by leveraging the network effort and the enabling technologies to "turbocharge" a particular supply chain. Leading manufacturing and service organizations in the automotive, aerospace, chemical, consumer goods, electronics, and pharmaceutical industries have already increased profits and shareholder value through the supply chain strategies and solutions outlined in this book. They are now seeking even higher levels of success. To illustrate the possibilities, let us envision a future that every company can pursue. We will consider each step along this journey toward building a powerful value chain constellation with rewards for each partner firm.

This journey begins with the assumption that firms aspiring to Level IV have some form of enterprisewide planning system in place, backed by an electronic, error-free order fulfillment system, so that a collective focus can be brought to cross-functional and cross-organizational issues. The typical organizational goal of profitable growth must be expanded to embrace systems that differentiate the firm and its allies from competing networks. The goal is achieved by an intelligent synthesis of individual firms' best systems and the customization of features that bring products and services to targeted markets better than any other network.

United efforts may be used to move an entire industry forward. Efficient health-care response (EHCR), efficient food service consumer response (EFCR), and several industries' focus on collaborative planning, forecasting, and replenishment (CPFAR) are excellent examples of such a combined effort. The Automotive Industry Action Group (AiAG) has sponsored and initiated an industrywide standards-based network (a budding extranet) for the automobile industry. Termed ANX, for Automobile Network Exchange, this extranet is an excellent launching pad for assembling potential value chain constellations.

> *The goal is achieved by an intelligent synthesis of individual firms' best systems and the customization of features that bring products and services to targeted markets better than any other network.*

However, as any process moves forward to protect the industry in general or to position it better for survival, a few of the industry members will attempt to use common lessons and improvements to enhance their individual success. As seen in the past, the industrywide effort may stall because members of a pilot team fear they will lose proprietary information or a market lead by sharing their know-how with competitors in their industry. My experience is that companies pursuing such cooperative efforts have nothing to fear if they form alliances with firms whose business philosophies and cultures are compatible with their own. Because most large competitors in an industry are close to the same position, they already know a great deal about one another's "secrets." Modern extranets also feature built-in "firewalls" that protect valuable proprietary information.

A feasible alternative is to form a core study group with support from a neutral industry organization. This core group recruits suppliers, distributors, and a focused customer to participate in a pilot effort aimed at creating a new business model for the industry, detailing the kind of innovative systems that could generate savings and attractive features for the targeted consumers. If care is taken to protect proprietary information and to prevent premature application of the findings, this pilot can achieve the kind of definition needed. It can also identify the improvement processes that could not be understood or pursued by the same firms working independently. The members of this pilot group and other constellations formed after presentation of the findings later apply the results of their pilot to gain an edge, working much closer with partner organizations to deliver products and services more effectively in concert.

Whether industry-sponsored or promoted by a nucleus firm, the value chain constellation emerges as an alliance among organizations with a similar vision. The constellation focuses on meeting the classic supply chain objective: offering the right combination of data, products, and services to customers and consumers at the right time and place and at the right price. Available-to-promise is an important feature of this alliance, backed with the lowest total delivered cost. At this final stage, a vision of future success goes beyond imagination to take on the appearance of reality—a dynamic approach to seamless, integrated supply chain management. To achieve this reality, the partners in the alliance must embrace a number of key elements:

▶ A focus on the Internet as a vital medium of communication
▶ Rapid, interactive, and successful product design and introduction
▶ Global available-to-promise capability with completely visible inventory
▶ Ability to assemble, build, or configure diverse components into a finished order
▶ Features of mass customization in the finished offering
▶ A glass pipeline for viewing availability and flow of goods and services
▶ Analytical and financial feedback loops that accurately measure progress
▶ Real-time "what if?" planning and simulation
▶ Flexible planning and execution to meet customer needs
▶ Zero working capital
▶ Continuous learning and improvement

▶ New Concepts and New Approaches to Business

With these parameters in mind, our journey of imagination begins in the design and development sector. In our reverie, innovations become a key means of marketplace differentiation. The value chain constellation must introduce new consumable products and services in the shortest possible time with a high probability of success. The constellation supports such innovative collaboration through information technology that provides the right data, in the right format, to the right places at the right times.

Exhibit 11.1 illustrates an interlinked infrastructure focused on bringing new designs and products to market quickly and effectively. Design and engineering changes driven by customer or consumer preferences are entered into a simulation model. Prototype designs are generated with help from key suppliers and other external sources, all transmitting ideas quickly and efficiently through high-speed electronic links. Product developers guide the introductions at every critical step, particularly where totally new products are required, but they work closely with constellation partners to speed the process and ensure higher probabilities of success. Designers work closely with purchasing managers to keep parts suppliers linked into the process to minimize delays and share design and production issues openly. Most important, planning time is condensed throughout the design and prototyping process through constant on-line feedback.

At this stage, it is essential for all constellation partners involved in marketing changes or new product introductions to be fully integrated with efforts to serve customers and consumers in the targeted market segments. Customer-focused teams will serve as a catalyst to manage the details of bringing the new ideas to fruition, extending their efforts into such nontraditional areas as influencing demand, establishing pricing, and (in some industries) designing promotion processes.

When the simulation model indicates that the product or change is ready, a prototype is released to production to make certain it is

EXHIBIT 11.1
Rapid Design, Development, and Change

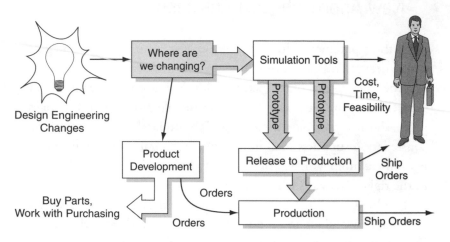

manufacturing-friendly and can flow through the supply chain efficiently. The external partners remain linked during this phase, especially those on the supply side (ensuring that design and manufacturing are compatible) and in the channel of distribution (guarding against waste in working capital and delivery processes), actively planning the introduction and promotion. By the time build orders are entered, the parts are ready, the system of delivery has been tested, cost and time and feasibility have all been accounted for, and the consumer receives the new market offering as the result of a seamless flow of activities. Inventories are matched to expected initial results and are coordinated with actual consumption.

The operations functions draw on flexible capabilities in order to respond rapidly to the mass customization features desired by consumers. Customers will receive products in various categories—make-to-order, assemble- or finish-to-order, or make-to-stock. These decisions regarding market segmentation will be made by the constellation. Postponement of finished goods without extra costs will be a feasible prospect because of the flexible features worked out by network members across the full supply chain. This strategy of committing resources to specific customer segments and targeted consumers will be crucial to the constellation's overall competitive advantage.

▶ Response Without Extra Cost

Imagine the power of immediate efficient consumer response (ECR), not just in principle but in fact as a key to marketplace differentiation. The value chain constellation will move beyond merely discussing consumer-based response to making it a reality in which many good things happen:

▶ Data from the point of consumption drives supply chain response across the full network.

▶ Consumers exercise their right to have products and services customized to their exact needs, and the constellation responds rapidly to meet those needs.

▶ Customers and consumers verify cost and product availability electronically.

▶ Products arrive at the point of consumption in the shortest possible time and in the highest possible quality, with the minimum amount of inventory to make the system work.

▶ Near-total flexibility is achieved in the network of supply without incurring unrecoverable costs.

At this stage, information technology is now interenterprise, linking all constellation partners' intranet systems to meet customer needs and actual consumer demand. Internet and message-based extranet communications allow the total planning and delivery system to respond rapidly and efficiently, without waste. The driver becomes consumption-driven supply chain response. Systems are integrated and work from actual consumption data, not forecasts. At every point in the network, optimized techniques (for example, dynamic and collaborative supply planning, business resource planning, sales force automation, and order configuration) are applied to control and speed delivery of the right products and services to the right consumers and the right time.

Electronic commerce now enables an advanced supply chain with clear advantages:

▶ Customers, suppliers, manufacturers, retailers, and distributors are connected in a virtual electronic enterprise that appears seamless to the ultimate consumer.

▶ Technology facilitates both information sharing and the necessary business transactions, without error.

▶ Technology changes the way constellation partners communicate and conduct business, creating new levels of understanding and trust.

▶ Companies in a virtual supply chain maintain technological superiority together to sustain competitive superiority.

Imagine that these benefits can be achieved with almost zero working capital, as illustrated in Exhibit 11.2. The ability to reduce necessary working capital almost to zero begins with dedication to a total pull system. Strategic forecasts are used to establish vendor-owned and -managed strategic inventory, but the levels are supported with on-line information regarding what is being pulled from the system. Guesswork is replaced by real-time data. The suppliers work hard to optimize available capacity and use of mutual assets. Daily throughput is optimized because the sales order demand is matched with supply on a dynamic basis. Replenishment comes from min/max inventories that can be reduced to the lowest feasible level because interactive planning systems eliminate the need for extra buffers and safety stocks. Distributors move parts, components, or finished goods to customers, who then transfer payments electronically based on advance shipping notices. Under this scenario, stagnation and hidden inventory are replaced by a smooth and efficient flow of product and service to the consumer and by Internet-transmitted transactions and payments that reduce each constituent's working capital needs.

▶ World-Class Business Interactions

When business is conducted in this way, simultaneous improvements in business interactions benefit all constituents. A network system is in place, moving the linked organizations from their current model of internal and independent excellence, where information and

EXHIBIT 11.2
Zero Working Capital

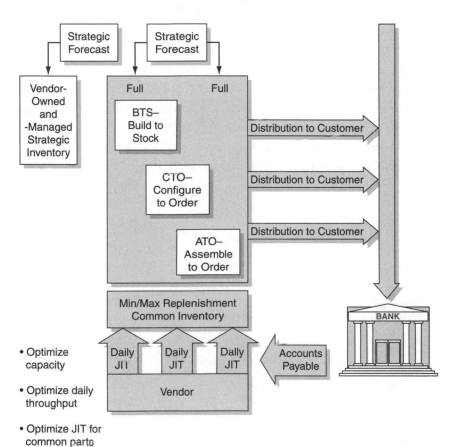

• Optimize capacity

• Optimize daily throughput

• Optimize JIT for common parts

Note: JIT, just-in-time processing.

upgrade paths do not support synchronous functionality across an entire value chain, to a condition where all areas of the interenterprise are maintained at the same level of improvement and are continuously upgraded. The processes of product development, demand management, order fulfillment, production planning, purchasing, manufacturing and conversion, inventory management, logistics, and delivery are under integrated network control. Financial reporting verifies the efficiency of the interactions and constantly documents higher levels of improvement.

Now imagine the glass pipeline, from raw material supplies to finished goods, in which inventories and product flow are visible at any time and any place in the value chain. Parts and products can be stopped, slowed, redirected, or speeded en route, depending on actual market conditions and consumer preferences. Inventory levels are known with great accuracy and can be managed at any point in the supply chain. The speed of movement is optimized for parts and products—nothing goes too quickly or too slowly; rather, everything moves in response to actual consumption.

Imagine that the network has advanced to the point where there is continuous and rapid learning, as shown in Exhibit 11.3. Under these

EXHIBIT 11.3
Continuous and Rapid Learning

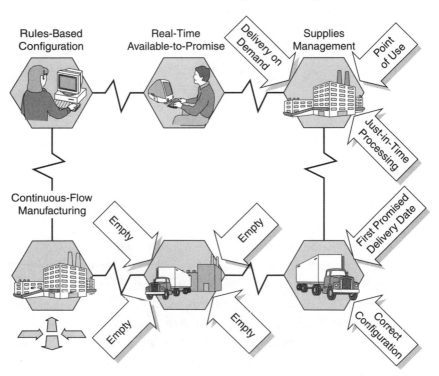

Multifunctional feedback loops result in
a rapid supply chain environment

conditions, the Internet-connected constituents have on-line, multi-directional feedback loops that result in rapid supply chain response and improvement. A rules-based configuration is used to implement available-to-promise information and to support continuous-flow manufacturing in real time. Management of supplies is under system control, deliveries are made to meet demand, and just-in-time operations function at the highest possible level to match the right point of use. The goods stored in warehouses shrink to what flows over a cross-dock, and first-promised delivery dates are met in the correct configuration at levels approaching 100 percent. Across this web of interaction, any failures can be quickly identified and remedied because learning is rapid and continuous. In short, the network is as close to optimal as is feasible with the corresponding technology.

As a complementary part of the vision, consider that a virtual corporation has been created, made up of formerly independent firms that are now linked as partners working together to secure profitable revenue growth. As Exhibit 11.4 illustrates, this corporation, which can source from anywhere on the globe, will use whatever part of the constellation is most effective to ship product anywhere in the world and does so through the most effective and smoothest-functioning network in the industry. In this virtual entity, suppliers act as buyers,

EXHIBIT 11.4
The Virtual Corporation

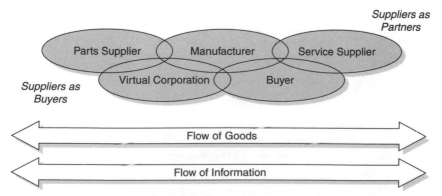

*Suppliers as buyers, supplies as partners, manufacturers as suppliers . . .
combinations are unlimited in virtual corporations.*

suppliers as partners, manufacturers as suppliers—an unlimited set of combinations make the network function as a virtual corporation dedicated to serving specific markets and consumers.

Imagine next that this virtual corporation has become so efficient at asset utilization that there is little, if any, static capital, as illustrated in Exhibit 11.5. Aging accounts receivable disappear because payment upon receipt is automatic and electronic. Standard lead times are minimized because production times are flexible and matched with actual demand. Finished goods inventory is at a minimum because goods are configured close to the point of sale and with great accuracy. Late shipments are a thing of the past because on-time delivery has reached 100 percent, and the time value of money becomes an important factor as funds are released for more important purposes.

EXHIBIT 11.5
Fully Utilized Capital

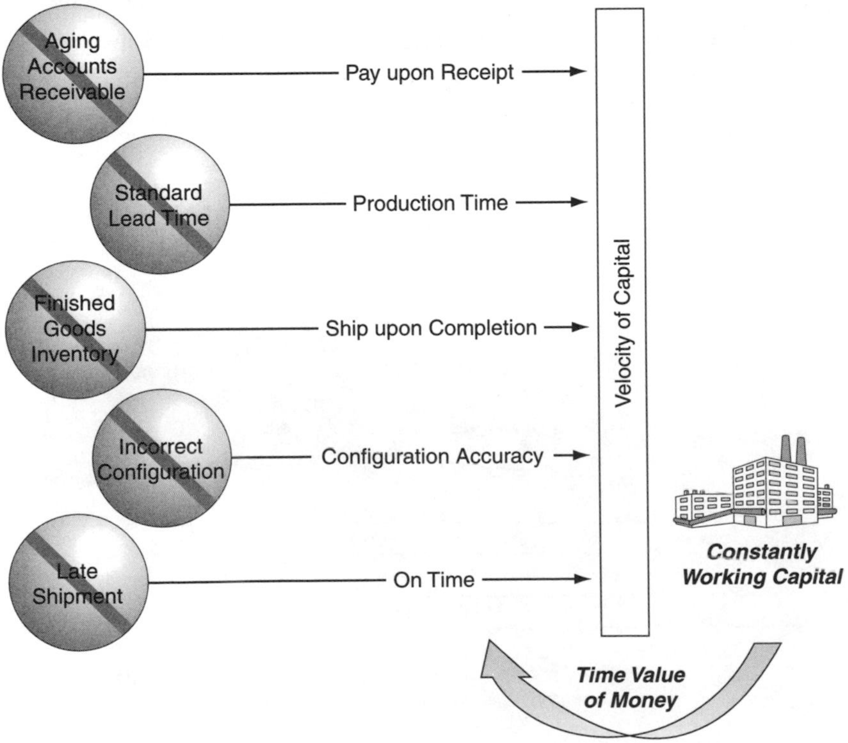

The new system will include short and predictable lead times because just-in-time delivery is real across the constellation. Lead times will be based on real production capacities that have been greatly enhanced through the interactive material and factory time data. Bills of material will be fully exploded to an infinite breadth and the routing examined electronically for capacity availability before committing available raw materials, work in process, and finished goods to available-to-promise status. Intelligent systems will release parts from internal and external suppliers at the last possible moment, and demand changes will be accommodated instantly. Order fulfillment will be an on-line, visible process, removing all excuses for stockouts. *Just-in-time* will be a watchword of all the suppliers who are part of the product bundling process and who no longer work in ignorance of what is being pulled from the systems. These suppliers, moreover, will be making valuable contributions to continuously improving the entire system of supply.

> Just-in-time *will be a watchword of all the suppliers who are part of the product bundling process and who no longer work in ignorance of what is being pulled from the systems.*

Imagine now that instant point-of-sale information is flowing in a circular fashion among the channel partners to assist in all aspects of replenishment, as shown in Exhibit 11.6. This information flow will document the fastest- and slowest-selling items. Inventory turns will be monitored on a real-time basis anywhere in the network. The rate of sale will be accessible on an hourly basis by any member of the constellation. Replenishment requests will be on-line, accessible, and responded to on a round-the-clock basis. Demand previously considered "perishable" because the system could not respond quickly enough will be turned into active orders. Orders that would formerly go to a competing network because only partial shipments could be made will be converted into on-time shipments with full fill rates.

▶ Fulfillment Arena: The Globe

Imagine that all this activity results in a global approach to localization. Standardized products are built to a common level for rapid

EXHIBIT 11.6
Instant Point-of-Sale Information from Channel Partners

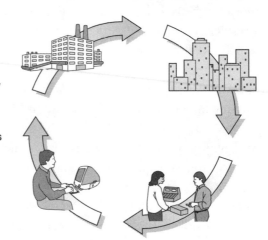

Instant information flow
• Fast-selling items
• Inventory
• Rate of sale
• Replenishment requests

transfer anywhere in the world so that they can be locally configured, completed, and shipped to the consumer. As fast as the local outlet (which could be halfway around the globe) can process quotes, deal with currency differences, establish pricing, deal with credit, and arrange the import-export details, the standard product and customized features are brought to the point of final assembly. Mass customization is achieved on a worldwide basis.

Market leadership will be achieved as a true consolidation of effort takes place, exhibiting mastery over those competing networks that have weaker relationships among partners. Highly effective business practices will become common expectations of the consumers who become loyal to the constellation. The number of suppliers, manufacturers, distributors, and retailers will shrink because some cannot make the cut at this stage. Disintermediation (the removal of non-value-adding intermediaries to the supply chain) is laid to rest by this time because the best constituent is doing what has to be done, often bypassing traditional links in the distribution channel.

At the same time, some partners will perform new roles as they pursue "offensive positioning" to develop new market positions. Distributors will no longer worry over their role in the constellation because they will serve specific market segments that cannot be served efficiently by more direct means. Markets and channels will be clearly defined, not in a state of crossover use and confusion, so that the distributor becomes an appropriate link in the system for certain market segments. Distributors will provide the catalog information, perform the order fulfillment, and make deliveries to customers and consumers too remote or too specialized for efficient handling by the manufacturer. The glass pipeline will facilitate this distribution function because the flow of materials and products will be completely transparent. No major network will be able to meet all consumer needs in a market without some form of distributor assistance.

> **No major network will be able to meet all consumer needs in a market without some form of distributor assistance.**

To compete successfully, smart organizations have already solidified the value chain constellations, demonstrating a superior way of supplying and servicing the markets of tomorrow. The constellations will manage a system of virtual distribution with very clear roles for each partner. They are leveraging an instantaneous information flow into unprecedented and unbeatable levels of response. Their direct links with suppliers, customers, and consumers transfer real-time data, enabling shared processes to achieve levels of performance previously thought to be impossible. Companies unprepared for this type of interaction will simply be unable to compete.

▶ Electronic Wave to the Future

To complement this portion of the reverie, imagine seamless integration made possible through three systems of information connection. As explained in Chapter 9, at the center is an *intranet,* a private system containing all the data of importance for optimizing use of assets and resources. Portions will be shared with other intranets for the purpose of having a glass pipeline of information, distinguishing the capability of the established value chain constellation. At the extremities of the intranet will be the *Internet,* the public system that is used by the members of the constellation to reach and serve the intended final consumers. Spanning both systems will be a public but privileged *extranet,* used by a value chain constellation to gain the desired competitive edge in the market of choice. This last system is the feature that will differentiate one network from its competitors.

There are two options regarding the construction of this seamless integration. The *advanced linear model* can be used for a network in which the constituents prefer to operate as peers with a single market and consumer focus. Exhibit 11.7 illustrates this concept. From the initial point of supply to the final point of consumption, the members of the linear value chain constellation will join to compete together more effectively. Suppliers will be using the privileged extranet to help develop new materials in support of new products. The downstream connections between suppliers and manufacturers are attempting to develop the "white space," the potentially valuable but unused capabilities of existing assets and resources, in order to bring new products and services to market.

Integrated solutions that positively affect processes, products, or services are sought. Alternative channels are explored, using the Internet, making certain that the best response is achieved at the lowest cost. Profitable new sales are developed through the network as sales leadership strategies are defined and pursued with the help of all constituents. The result is a totally new business system, enhancing the probability of success for the value chain constellation. Order management activities and important data flow bidirectionally in the extranet because each firm is using its intranet capability to provide important information that cuts cycle time and minimizes inventories and expediting.

Across the bottom of Exhibit 11.7 are some of the key elements of success. Product development, distribution efficiency, and product replenishment reach new levels of competitive distinction. Order fulfillment and marketing strategy are now strengths rather than limitations. New business development pervades the value chain constellation. Beneath these factors is a calibration scale to mark the progress of the network as it moves inexorably toward the desired position of attaining an advantage over competing networks.

In the *circular* or *mushroom model,* shown in Exhibit 11.8, the nucleus firm has taken a central position using its viable intranet,

EXHIBIT 11.7
The Advanced Linear Supply Chain

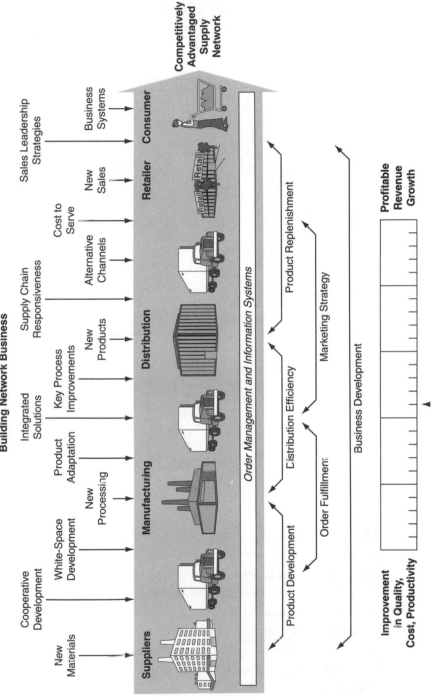

Building Network Business

| New Materials | Cooperative Development | White-Space Development | New Processing | Product Adaptation | Integrated Solutions | Key Process Improvements | New Products | Supply Chain Responsiveness | Alternative Channels | Cost to Serve | New Sales | Sales Leadership Strategies | Business Systems |

Suppliers — **Manufacturing** — **Distribution** — **Retailer** — **Consumer**

Competitively Advantaged Supply Network

Order Management and Information Systems

Product Development — Distribution Efficiency — Marketing Strategy

Order Fulfillment — Product Replenishment

Business Development

Improvement in Quality, Cost, Productivity

Profitable Revenue Growth

EXHIBIT 11.8
The Advanced Nucleus Unit Model of Supply Chain Management

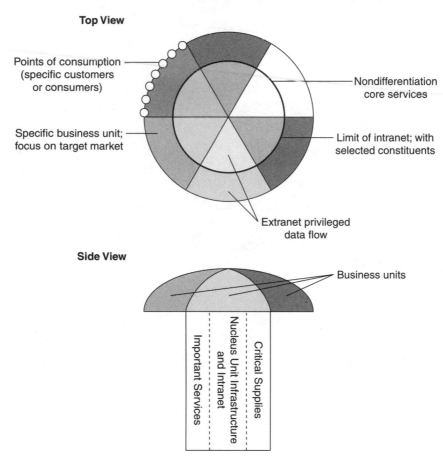

Top View

Points of consumption (specific customers or consumers)

Nondifferentiation core services

Specific business unit; focus on target market

Limit of intranet; with selected constituents

Extranet privileged data flow

Side View

Business units

Important Services

Nucleus Unit Infrastructure and Intranet

Critical Supplies

where internal data are being used to maximize benefits across all functions at the ultimate level of sophistication. With the additional aid of the open and inexpensive public Internet as a crucial means of expanding the capabilities of the intranet, linked partners are given access to an extranet. That communication system is still public but has become privileged through custom-designed features. A single, acceptable program language is used to support object abstraction for dynamic, fast, and extremely flexible connectivity and response. With a specific focus for each business unit, the nucleus firm reaches out with the help of its key allies to serve the ultimate customers and consumers of choice.

The illustration in Exhibit 11.8 is presented in two dimensions to detail the concept. Beginning with the side view, the nucleus unit's infrastructure and intranet form the core of the mushroom-shaped model. A consumer product company like Kraft Foods or Procter & Gamble, or an industrial firm like Du Pont, sits at the core of the constellation. This position is taken because of the enormous strength of the brand names or proprietary strength of the central element in the products to be produced (such as nylon or Spandex for Du Pont; Tide, Cheer, or Pampers for P&G; Velveeta or Maxwell House for Kraft Foods). Around this core position are arrayed the supplies needed to make the proprietary products. This part of the column could include raw materials like flour, sweeteners, starch, chemicals, food products, and important subassemblies and components. Around the rest of the column would be important services such as energy and transportation. The supporting column would be specific to each nucleus unit but should contain the limited number of key network constituents upon which the efficient functioning of the constellation will depend.

The existing intranet of the nucleus unit, which has by now been developed to a leading-edge position (free of errors, covering the entire order fulfillment process, with flexible connectivity), is opened to these select members, allowing these firms access to important (and previously proprietary) data under conditions of security. The nondifferentiating core services are excluded, simply because they offer no value to the external partners, but are used for such internal strategic services as accounts receivable, accounts payable, recruiting, and other human resource functions. The differentiating services are included, however, to gain an advantage that can derive from direct access to information crucial to cycle time and efficiency of distribution. The need for forecasting is abolished because the constituents are on-line with one another, sharing demand and supply information on a real-time basis. Access to manufacturing schedules is provided to link supply with demand and eliminate the guesswork in order processing.

Moving to the top view, each separate business unit now spreads out from the core services toward the markets of choice. In these slices of the mushroom, a business unit begins using the Internet to access consumers of choice more efficiently and to help retail customers gain orders from the targeted segment. The nucleus unit maintains the Internet system, which provides useful data for all business units. Within each pie segment or business unit area of focus, an extranet is created with the constituents necessary to complete the value chain constellation. At the tips of the pie segment (shown as the small circles) are the specific customers or consumers of choice.

An elaboration will be helpful in understanding this mushroom model. Exhibit 11.9 presents a specific example for the paper industry. Beginning with the side view, the nucleus unit (which could be, say, International Paper, Georgia-Pacific, or Weyerhaeuser) has an intranet built around its forests, paper mills, and paper machines, producing a wide variety of brown and white paper products. This intranet is cross-functional and brings an intraenterprise communication system to a point where any important data will be accessible and reliable. Supporting the network (the column of the mushroom) are suppliers of such critical supplies as trees (contract farmers), pulp, and chemicals (such as Du Pont or Dow). Also supporting the network are important services like the energy provider, railroads, and trucking organizations. These organizations are linked together conceptually and technologically through the sharing of portions of the nucleus intranet and connections to important parts of the supporting firms' internal data systems.

The various business units are described in the top view. The central intranet is extended to the edge of the Internet by giving key suppliers and service providers access to the portion of the intranet that will facilitate their support. The Internet is used to assist the combined business strategies in reaching the consumers of choice. Diaper Pulp is focused on a specific market segment that could include P&G, Kimberly-Clark, and other manufacturers of disposable diapers. In concert with these customers, the network is trying to offer new features, reduce total costs, or provide innovative improvements that take business from less agile and forward-thinking networks.

EXHIBIT 11.9
Example of a Mushroom Model in the Paper Industry

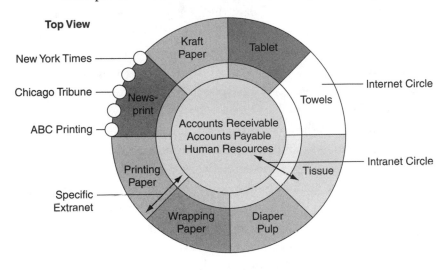

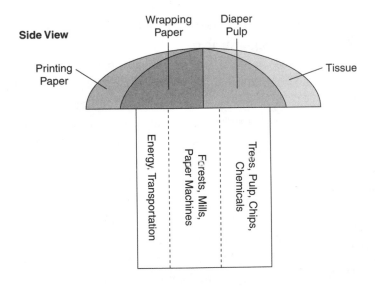

Printing Paper would be focused on producers of annual reports, major magazines, and so forth. The Newsprint unit is chasing such customers as the *New York Times,* the *Chicago Tribune,* and the printers of local or regional newspapers. In these cases, the focus is on specific paper products customers. A consumer product nucleus unit might have Kroger, Safeway, or HEB Foods as targets in the grocery sector of the mushroom. The purpose is to join forces and use joint resources in this focused segment to optimize the use of assets and people, relying on the competitively advantaged technology network to share information and sell to the consumers of choice.

A specific extranet is created between the business unit and the constituents that make up the pie segment of the model that goes from the internal intranet to the limits of the Internet. This is the privileged connection that allows the constituents to use an open and inexpensive medium of communication to facilitate all interactions. It is this Web connection, for example, that helps the paper manufacturer work with the newspapers to find ways to increase circulation with the targeted consumers or to help the diaper manufacturer move more diapers in a global arena.

With these models in mind, imagine, finally, that technology has removed the fundamental business barriers. Every important member of the constellation is in effect a next-door neighbor because of the instant access and connectivity. Any member of the value chain constellation can connect with another constituent anywhere on the globe around the clock and around the calendar. Higher transaction volumes are not just possible; they are happening with greater frequency. Electronic commerce has banished the time and geography constraints. The content is fully digitized, and replication is easy. Time, reach, focus, and form are no longer constraining the business interactions. Trust reaches new highs because all partners have worked together in achieving the value chain constellation.

> *Every important member of the constellation is in effect a next-door neighbor because of the instant access and connectivity.*

Consider at the conclusion of our dream journey the following benefits of this new method of advanced supply chain management:

▶ Rapid product introduction and differentiation, with the best times to market

▶ Almost total flexibility in the chain of supply, with almost no static capital

▶ Customers, suppliers, manufacturers, distributors, and retailers sharing information vital to their mutual success in a secure and reliable manner

▶ Minimized need for working capital, facilitated by optimal inventory levels

▶ Simultaneous and ongoing improvement of all areas of the interenterprise network

▶ Total visibility across the pipeline connecting the network constituents

▶ Multidirectional feedback loops for rapid response and improvement

▶ Virtual alliances with key constituents in a business framework that ensures future profits, growth, and competitive success

Now, stop imagining and go out and turn the turbocharged supply chain into a reality!

Bibliography

Arntzen, Bruce, Daniel Mulgrew, and Garry Sjolander. "Redesigning 3M's Worldwide Produce Supply Chains." *Supply Chain Management Review,* Winter 1998, pp. 16–27.

Bauer, Michael, and Jim Sinex. "Optimized Customer Care: Streamlining Customer Care for Growth and Efficiency." Paper presented at the Electronic Commerce for Chemicals Conference, Computer Sciences Corporation, Philadelphia, June 25, 1998.

Biciocchi, Steve. "E-Wave: Driving Retail Strategy in the 21st Century." Eighth Annual Retail Technology Study. Cleveland, Ohio: Computer Sciences Corporation, 1998.

Copacino, William C. "Supply Chain Management." American Productivity and Inventory Control Society, 1997.

Cortese, Amy, and Marcia Stepanek. "Good-Bye to Fixed Pricing? How Electronic Commerce Could Create the Most Efficient Market of Them All." *Business Week,* May 4, 1998, pp. 71–84.

Dalton, Gregory. "Intranets, Internets: Both Sides Now." *Information Week,* May 4, 1998, p. 104.

Deloitte and Touche Consulting Group. "The North American Survey of Trends in Supply Chain Management," 1998.

Grant, Alan, and Leonard Schlesinger. "Realize Your Customers' Full Potential." *Harvard Business Review,* September-October 1995, pp. 59–72.

Green, Heather, Gail De George, and Amy Barrett. "The Virtual Mall Gets Real." *Business Week,* January 26, 1998, pp. 90–91.

Hof, Robert, Gary McWilliams, and Gabrielle Saveri. "The 'Click Here' Economy." *Business Week,* June 22, 1998, pp. 122–128.

Horwitt, Elisabeth. "Casting a Wider Net." *Computerworld,* June 8, 1998, pp. 14–16.

Kupfner, Andrew. "4 Forces That Will Shape the Internet." *Fortune,* July 6, 1998, pp. 93–100.

Levitt, Jason. "The Internet Presents . . ." *Information Week,* September 15, 1997, pp. 61–68.

Manchester, Philip. "Supply and Internet Demand." *Financial Post,* October 18, 1997, p. 47.

Martin, James D. "CEOs and Logistics: Thinking out of the Box." *Inbound Logistics,* June 1997, pp. 22–28.

Mentzer, John T. *Sales Forecasting Management.* Thousand Oaks, Calif.: Sage, 1997.

Payne, Jason. "Creating a Virtual Enterprise Through Internet/Intranet Solutions." Internal paper for XATA Corporation.

Reinhardt, A. "What Could Whip the World Wide Wait." *Business Week,* February 16, 1998, p. 83.

Sheridan, John H. "Kaizen Blitz." *Industry Week,* September 1, 1997, pp. 18–28.

Stein, Tom. "Extending ERP." *Information Week,* June 15, 1998, pp. 75–82.

Stein, Tom. "Orders from Chaos." *IW Magazine,* June 23, 1997, pp. 44–52.

Wilder, Clinton. "The Intermediaries Must Meet the Internet Challenge." *Information Week,* May 4, 1998, p. 3.

Wilder, Clinton. "Peer into the Net's Future." *Information Week,* May 4, 1998, pp. 6–11.

Index

About the Author

Charles C. Poirier is a partner with the National Supply Chain Practice of Computer Sciences Corporation (CSC), one of the world's largest information technology and management consulting firms. He is a regular contributor to domestic and international conferences and seminars on subjects ranging from supply chain optimization and electronic commerce to finding value throughout a business enterprise and its associated partnering opportunities.

Poirier has held a variety of management positions, including senior vice president of manufacturing and marketing at Tenneco, Inc., a *Fortune* 100 organization. His background includes direct management experience in productivity, quality control, cost containment, mergers and acquisitions, training, sales and marketing, and information technology.

His publications include *Business Partnering for Continuous Improvement* (Berrett-Koehler), *Avoiding the Pitfalls of Total Quality Management* (ASQC Press), and *Supply Chain Optimization* (Berrett-Koehler).

Berrett-Koehler Publishers

B ERRETT-KOEHLER is an independent publisher of books, periodicals, and other publications at the leading edge of new thinking and innovative practice on work, business, management, leadership, stewardship, career development, human resources, entrepreneurship, and global sustainability.

Since the company's founding in 1992, we have been committed to supporting the movement toward a more enlightened world of work by publishing books, periodicals, and other publications that help us to integrate our values with our work and work lives, and to create more humane and effective organizations.

We have chosen to focus on the areas of work, business, and organizations, because these are central elements in many people's lives today. Furthermore, the work world is going through tumultuous changes, from the decline of job security to the rise of new structures for organizing people and work. We believe that change is needed at all levels— individual, organizational, community, and global—and our publications address each of these levels.

We seek to create new lenses for understanding organizations, to legitimize topics that people care deeply about but that current business orthodoxy censors or considers secondary to bottom-line concerns, and to uncover new meaning, means, and ends for our work and work lives.

See next page for other books from Berrett-Koehler Publishers

Other leading-edge business books from Berrett-Koehler Publishers

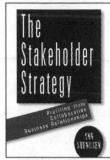

Stewardship

Choosing Service Over Self-Interest

Peter Block

BLOCK SHOWS HOW to recreate our workplaces by replacing self-interest, dependency, and control with service, responsibility, and partnership. He demonstrates how a far-reaching redistribution of power, privilege, and wealth will radically change all areas of organizational governance, and shows why this is our best hope to enable democracy to thrive.

Paperback, 288 pages, 3/96 • ISBN 1-881052-86-9 CIP
Item no. 52869-266 $16.95

Hardcover, 7/93 • ISBN 1-881052-28-1 CIP • **Item no. 52281-266 $27.95**

Getting to Resolution

Turning Conflict Into Collaboration

Stewart Levine

STEWART LEVINE gives readers an exciting new set of tools for resolving personal and business conflicts. Marriages run amuck, neighbors at odds with one another, business deals gone sour, and the pain and anger caused by corporate downsizing and layoffs are just a few of the conflicts he addresses.

Hardcover, 200 pages, 3/98 • ISBN 1-57675-005-1 CIP
Item no. 50051-266 $19.95

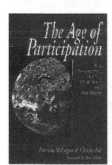

The Age of Participation

New Governance for the Workplace and the World

by Patricia McLagan and Christo Nel
foreword by Peter Block

PATRICIA McLAGAN and Christo Nel describe the massive transformation that is occurring in human institutions today. Blending theory and practice, providing numerous examples, and drawing on more than forty years of experience in over 200 organizations, McLagan and Nel describe what executives, managers, workers, labor unions, customers, and suppliers can do as part of a participative enterprise. In this practical, experience-based handbook, they look closely at every level of life in a participative organization and deflate the fears and misperceptions that can sabotage change.

Hardcover, 300 pages, 9/95 • ISBN 1-881052-56-7 CIP
Item no. 52567-266 $27.95

Available at your favorite bookstore, or call (800) 929-2929

Put the Leading-Edge
Business Practices You Read About
to Use in Your Work and in Your Organization

D O EVER YOU WISH there was a forum in your organization for discussing the newest trends and ideas in the business world? Do you wish you could explore the leading-edge business practices you read about with others in your company? Do you wish you could set aside a few hours every month to connect with like-minded coworkers or to get to know others in your business community?

If you answered yes to any of these questions, then the answer is simple: Start a business book reading group in your organization or business community. For step-by-step advice on how to do just that, visit the Berrett-Koehler website at <www.bkpub.com> and click on "Reading Groups." There you'll find specific guidelines to help in all aspects of creating a successful reading group—from locating interested participants to selecting books, and facilitating discussions.

These guidelines were created as part of the Business Literacy 2000 program launched by the Consortium for Business Literacy—a group of 19 business book publishers whose primary goal has been to promote the formation of business reading groups within corporations and business communities. Business Literacy 2000 is dedicated to providing you with tools to help you build a dialog with others in your company or business community, share ideas, build lasting relationships, and bring new ideas and knowledge to bear in your work and organizations.

For more information on the Business Literacy 2000 program, guidelines for starting a business book reading group, or to browse or download the study guides that are available for our books, please visit our website at: <www.bkpub.com>.

If you do not have internet access, you may request information by contacting us at:

Berrett-Koehler Publishers
450 Sansome St., Suite 1200
San Francisco, CA 94111
Fax (415) 362-2512
Email bkpub@bkpub.com

Please be sure to include your name, address, telephone number, and the information you would like to receive.